PRAISE FOR *THE BLUEPRINT*

Todd Bloomer has crafted a wonderful resource that will serve school leaders at any level of experience. This book is not just *The Blueprint* in title, but it is a mentor that you will revisit for continued insight, inspiration, and dynamic action.

Sean Gaillard
Principal, Author, Podcaster

Todd Bloomer's *The Blueprint* is a heartfelt and invaluable resource for educational administrators. Originally an email to his brother, Todd's passion and authenticity shine through, enriched by his extensive experience and personal stories. His emphasis on the first 30 days provides a clear roadmap for success, crucial for driving one's work. A key theme is his belief in strong school culture and being visible, especially to students, shaping his leadership approach through stakeholder feedback. Todd's advice on finding a tribe of mentors resonates deeply with me and speaks to its importance. This book is essential not only for new administrators but also for seasoned leaders seeking continuous growth.

Dominic Armano
Principal, Author

The Blueprint is a must read for any administrator at any stage of their career. Todd Bloomer provides applicable techniques based on tried-and-true methods along with his own experience. Bloomer is authentic in sharing both successes and failures so all can learn from him. The checklists and "What would Bloomer do?" reflective questions are most helpful.

Dr. Danielle Jackson
High School Principal

In *The Blueprint,* Todd Bloomer provides practical and heartfelt insight to ensure the success of what he calls "superhero" building administrators. Bloomer, currently an experienced HS Principal, shares his own perspective and recommended practical actions alongside the voices of numerous school leaders all across the state and nation gleaned through his interactions, experiences, and relationships. These actions provide the reader with a guide to shape positive culture in schools, in building meaningful relationships with students, staff, parents and mentors, and ultimately leads to an opportunity to find real joy in the difficult work of leadership. Anchored in an inspiring call to champion the work taking place in schools by our educators, *The Blueprint* is an excellent resource for all school leaders and is one I will be sharing with leaders I personally want to grow and develop.

Dana Bashara
28 year educator (former Teacher, Assistant Principal, Principal, HR Director, Communications Director, Assistant Superintendent)
Currently serving as Superintendent of Schools

The job of a school administrator can be lonely and sometimes overwhelming. The demands of the community, the school district, the campus staff, and the students can pull a new administrator in several directions at once. Along with learning the skills to be an effective administrator, we also need to learn how to balance our personal lives. This is where *The Blueprint* comes in. Todd Bloomer has created a thoughtful, easy-to-read guide with outstanding advice from his years of experience and several vignettes from other effective school leaders. This guide will be invaluable to new administrators and those who have been in the position and are looking to create a balance in their lives and careers. What a great investment in your success!

Martin Silverman
Retired Principal/Consultant/Coach/Author

In *The Blueprint*, Mr. Bloomer provides strategies for new and experienced school leaders, for those engaged in what he argues is among our society's greatest professions, that of educator and school leader. He gives practical advice for beginning a new principalship and building a campus culture, while also imploring leaders to take care of themselves. Throughout this project, Mr. Bloomer continued to lead his high school during a tumultuous time in our country's history. However, what is clear from reading this book is that Mr. Bloomer continues to lead from his heart with joy. Throughout his professional journey, he's shifted his practice and evolved as a leader - now he wants to share his blueprint with others wanting to do the same.

Enrique Alemán, Jr.
Lillian Radford Endowed Professor of Education, Trinity University

From his mentor to his boss and now admirer of his life's work, watching Todd grow into a leader of leaders has been an honor. *The Blueprint* is a culmination of the lessons he has learned along his leadership journey and chock full of advice for current or aspiring school leaders. Take time and read this! You will walk away a better leader.

Sean Maika
Superintendent

Doubt is one word that enters the minds of many school leaders when they are handed the keys to a school. Whether you are new to the profession or a veteran school leader, *The Blueprint*, by Todd Bloomer, will serve as a resource guide to help you navigate the challenges that leaders face daily. Filled with personal stories and anecdotes from his experience as a long-time school leader, Todd reminds us that we are never alone in this work.

Jimmy Casas
Educator, Leadership Coach, Author, Speaker

As a tenured administrator, I quickly connected with Principal Bloomer's book when I read, "your why is who you are as a leader, what you stand for and what you believe in." He brings to life real events that take place on a campus and creates a "how to" manual for all educators especially those who aspire to lead a school. If you are in the trenches or you are currently sitting in the main chair of a school, this is a must read so you can use *The Blueprint* for student success.

Josh Tovar
Principal

The Blueprint, by Todd Bloomer, offers a candid and practical resource for new school administrators stepping into leadership roles. Drawing on his experience as principal of Winston Churchill High School in San Antonio, TX, Bloomer outlines essential characteristics of effective school leadership. He navigates crucial topics like the first 30 days, transitioning between roles, and the importance of building authentic relationships. Bloomer addresses the often-overlooked aspect of isolation in leadership roles, advocating for a supportive network to counteract this challenge. With insights from principals nationwide, this manuscript provides a holistic guide invaluable to aspiring and current educational leaders alike.

Kenneth Washington
Executive Director Student Services Mesquite ISD

Todd Bloomer delivers in this one! *The Blueprint* includes practical insight from an experienced school leader. Throughout, Todd encourages educators to consider how they want to be perceived by their community. He provides tips for everything from leading your first 30 days as a school administrator to creating an environment everyone is proud of. This book provides the steps to follow so you can lead better than ever before.

Brandon Beck
Speaker, Author, Leadership Coach

What sets *The Blueprint* apart is Todd's ability to seamlessly intertwine his personal experiences with practical strategies for success. Through his heartfelt storytelling, he not only shares the ups and downs of his own journey but also provides invaluable lessons for aspiring school administrators and educators alike.

The Blueprint is not just a book; it is a roadmap for personal and professional growth. Todd Bloomer's insights and guidance will empower readers to become better school administrators, fostering positive change within their own educational communities. His book serves as a beacon of hope and inspiration, reminding us all of the crucial role that educators play in shaping the future.

Archie E. McAfee, Executive Director
Texas Association of Secondary School Principals, Austin, TX

THE BLUEPRINT
Survive and Thrive as a School Administrator

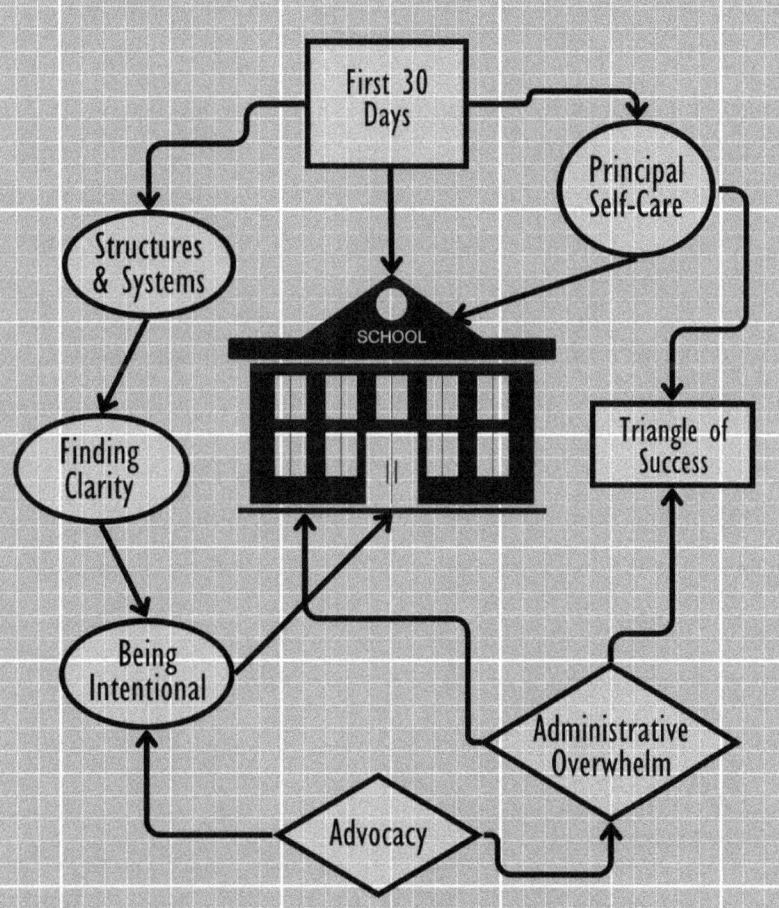

TODD M. BLOOMER

The Blueprint: Survive and Thrive as a School Administrator

Copyright © by Todd M. Bloomer
First Edition 2024

All rights reserved.

No part of this publication may be reproduced in any form, or by any means, electronic or mechanical, including photocopying, recording, or any information browsing, storage or retrieval system, without permission in writing from the publisher.

Road to Awesome, LLC.

To my wife, Sharon, my best friend and my ride-or-die!

I love the life we have.

Hey, kids! *The Blueprint* finally dropped.

TABLE OF CONTENTS

Foreword	1
Introduction	3
Chapter 1	9
The First Thirty Days	
Chapter 2	67
Find Your Tribe of Mentors	
Chapter 3	87
Establishing, Shaping, and Managing Campus Culture	
Chapter 4	121
Disrupting the Status Quo & Leading for Change	
Chapter 5	153
Hiring–Doing the Work Up Front So You Don't Have to Work on the Back End	
Chapter 6	177
Managing Your Time So it Doesn't Manage You. The Blueprint to Developing a Work Balance for You	
Chapter 7	201
Advice for Administrators-Don't Take My Word; Take Theirs	
Farewell	213
About the Author	215
How to Book Bloomer	216

FOREWARD

Dr. Lance Groppel
Deputy Superintendent of Administration
Tyler Independent School District, Tyler, Texas

The Blueprint is an excellent guide for anyone looking for a resource that gives tips and tricks to school leadership. The role of a principal has changed as drastically over the past twenty years as the students have changed during that time frame. The relationship with an adult is the most significant predictor of a student's success. As a campus principal, you must foster a culture that values this aspect of our job, and *The Blueprint* will help you create that culture.

I enjoyed meeting Todd during our time with Raise Your Hand Texas, specifically the Harvard Principals' Institute. Over the past ten years, I have learned and grown from his wisdom. Our collaborative dialogue, as well as many others, has led him to write *The Blueprint*. This book will help administrators of varying experience levels. As a first-year administrator, I would have appreciated a resource like this to help guide me through some of the trials and tribulations of being a first-year administrator. As an experienced educator, I now have a different view and understand the importance of growth and how others can help me improve my craft and, more importantly, my campus.

The job of the principal is challenging and lonely. The resources in *The Blueprint* are greatly helpful in creating new ideas and affirming my ideas about leading my campus. Many principals struggle with the need to bounce ideas off someone else, and *The Blueprint* will provide that for all principals. This affirmation will help lead to a thriving campus because a successful leader will be at the helm.

INTRODUCTION

About five years before *The Blueprint* was written, my brother was named an assistant principal at an elementary school in Texas. I wanted to share some advice with him so he would have a successful start to his career. So, I started writing him an email. The email grew from one page to two, then three, then four.

Soon, this became more than a simple email wishing my brother good luck and sharing a few tips with him. I divided the letter into sections – the first part covered his first month on the job, then I included a section about working on the campus culture. I also added advice I had received from parents through the years. And with that... *The Blueprint* was born.

Over the next five years, I occasionally revisited and worked on the book. Life got in the way, and very quickly, the book became a distant memory. Fast forward to 2023, and it was finished. Writing the *The Blueprint* was like the principalship – from successes to failures and everything in between, I poured my heart and soul into the project.

The Blueprint was rejected and rejected again. I almost gave up, but I am glad I didn't. I continued to share the manuscript with anyone who showed a remote interest. I compared it to an underground mixtape that circulated before being released or discovered. I was Run-DMC before meeting Rick Rubin. That is how I describe meeting Darrin Peppard, the person who agreed to publish my book.

This book is my administrative journey. From the joys of being appointed to my first principalship to debating walking away to reflecting fondly. Like an old man sharing wisdom with his grandchildren, I laid it all on the line. My experience had a purpose that could benefit and strengthen our profession. As Brené Brown, a noted leadership author, would say, "I have rumbled with vulnerability as I have laid it all on the line."

My goal is for *The Blueprint* to serve as a guide to address and overcome administrative overwhelm. Administrative overwhelm is a phenomenon that has swept through schools across the country. It is a fog-like plague that Stephen King might write about. It pushes veteran administrators out and propels unprepared principals into new positions.

I have been a principal for ten years. I have implemented systems and structures to assist me with the day-to-day responsibilities of being a building principal and fighting off the overload. But if I am being honest, administrative overwhelm is starting to get to me. I am having to work harder than I ever have before. On a daily basis, I must channel my energy and time into places I never have. I have been injured on the job and beat up on social media. One slip-up and I might become an administrative casualty. Many of my colleagues have left education citing many different reasons for their departure.

The terrible incident in Uvalde shook the world when twenty-one innocent children were massacred in their classrooms. Massacred. This is just one of the many tragedies that has made administrators ensure their school has police officers and locked doors and gates. They are also charged with ensuring students' mental health needs are met. This includes dealing with food insecurity, evictions, and homelessness. Administrators are tasked with combating drug use, including fighting vape devices that look like highlighters or cell phone chargers. Schools are expected to solve every issue or concern a student or family has.

Administrators are required to help with social media, including anonymous sites that ridicule students or "spill the tea." It also involves keeping track of students who make threats online to individuals or the school itself. Administrators deal with gender issues, pregnancy, and suicide outcries each week. Who would have thought that we would have to monitor who uses which bathroom when we earned our degree?

Have you noticed that I have not mentioned anything that is academically related?

In 2024, public education has been put in the crossfire of state politicians. We have been made out to be the bad guy – Public Enemy #1. Legislatures have accused librarians of having porn in the library. Elected officials, many of whom have not attended a public school in thirty or more years, blame teachers for indoctrination. These same officials are trying to destroy public education through the mask of vouchers or parent choice.

I wrote this book to share that you are not alone in your journey as an administrator or in sometimes feeling overwhelmed and inadequate. We have all been there; depending on the day and time, I might be there right now. These feelings come in waves. Through trial and error, structures, systems, clarity, hope, and stories, I will lay out a blueprint for you to survive and thrive.

The Blueprint is meant for aspiring administrators, teacher-leaders, current administrators, and central office personnel. It was also written for teachers, community members, and even students in leadership positions because what is discussed within the book should and can be implemented in every school across the globe.

The stories that are shared throughout the book make you reflect, make you ponder, and make you laugh. I also hope that each chapter assists you in your leadership journey. We are all in this game together, so let's band together and change the game. We are better together.

A Note from my brother, Sean Bloomer, High School Assistant Principal

Having a brother who is several steps ahead of me on the road to administration has been a lifesaver. Whenever something hits the fan, having him just a text away has been great. Whatever I'm experiencing, he has walked it numerous times. Sometimes, his guidance is pure big brother. What advice did he give me before my first principal interview? Make sure your fly is up. Thanks, bro! Big Help! But he guides with passion and purpose whenever it is about kids.

Whether handling difficult teachers, helping me keep my sense of humor, or navigating a parental minefield, I can count on my brother to get me through it!

CHAPTER 1
The First Thirty Days

Welcome to the club, my friend! Your first thirty days on the job are the key to a successful year!

Your administrative honeymoon lasts for the first thirty days. Utilizing social media will help you during your transition. Challenge yourself to document the first thirty days on social media. Post a picture of every day you are on the job, of what it is like to be on your campus. Use social media to allow your community to get to know you.

I consider myself a "glass half full" kind of guy. My book is filled with optimism about our profession and paints a picture of the joys of school leadership. But I start with a stark warning: *Nothing truly prepares you to sit in the big chair.*

I wasn't prepared when I moved from the classroom to the assistant principal's chair. I was ready but not prepared because nothing truly prepares you for the big chair except sitting in the big chair. This job is unlike any other. The demands, expectations, and responsibilities change each year, and your job description might say TBD. Everything is your fault and nothing is because of your leadership. With all that said, I have a collection of lessons, truths, and suggestions that can ease the transition and put you on the path to success.

You might be new to the campus or have been promoted from within. You might be a current principal getting ready to begin a new year. No matter the situation, this is an exciting and wonderful time! So, let's start with the positives.

If this is your first job as an administrator, enjoy the congratulatory texts and well wishes. You have earned them. Take a few moments to soak it all in. Close your eyes, kick your feet on the table, and let the moment sink in. Let your hair down, and bask in your accomplishment.

Throughout my years in administration, I have worked with numerous administrators on my team and hundreds of others in my district. I have seen examples of fantastic leadership and miserable failure. I have also had tremendous success and moments of extreme failure throughout my career. It is this knowledge that I want to share.

Our profession cannot afford poor leadership. Our students, community, and staff deserve to be led by empathic, creative, and innovative administrators. Through my tenure, I have learned that the campus principal holds the magical power to transform a campus, a community, and a faculty. The principal is a game-changer!

From the moment you are announced in your position, you are in the critical observational interview during which the staff, community, and students observe and evaluate if your words and actions match. The first thirty days on the job will be crucial to the success of your year. Staff members will come by and say hello. They will smile and offer help, support, and advice. But they will also be watching and listening to everything that comes out of your mouth. They will monitor your body language and what you do during the day. This is probably as close as you will ever be to having a paparazzi or understanding what it is like to be a celebrity. The conversations in the teacher's lounge and parking lot will be about YOU: your actions, words, and body language.

"On the first day, they'll start forming their opinions on whether they like you and if you are believable. In the first week, they'll watch you like a hawk. You'll have to make sure you are consistent in greeting, welcoming and acknowledging staff and students, and treating everyone the same. In the first month, they'll decide if you mean what you say and if you can apply that knowledge in a way that they understand."

Crystal Romero-Mueller
Administrator, Houston, TX

If you are a current administrator reading this book, the topics and discussions are relevant, yearly reminders of our profession's requirements. This is a beautiful self-reflection for the first thirty days of each year. When I transitioned from middle to high school principal, I reflected on this chapter as I developed my entry plan. I re-read my blueprint to ensure I was on the right track.

I often wished that when I first moved from the classroom to join the administrative team, I would have had someone stress just how important these first thirty days were. Because of that, I have created a checklist crucial to your success. I share this list with you because I want you to be successful! Our children need strong leadership to guide their schools.

The checklist is designed to help you manage your first thirty days. Each item on the list has been selected for particular reasons. I share very personal stories that are easily relatable for you to be successful. While this book is designed for the 21st-century principal, the practices are tried and true, and this advice can stand the test of time. To this day, I still reflect on this chapter at the beginning of each semester.

I have divided the list into two sections. The first part deals with mindsets you must develop or cultivate for success. These mindsets require you to spend time in thought. This might require re-reading at times, making notes, and deep self-reflection. The second part contains items that you can complete or schedule. These are easier to grasp yet just as important.

Here is the blueprint to success and your entry plan for a successful beginning to any school year.

PART ONE

1. UNDERSTAND WHO YOU ARE REPLACING

I am unique. (Those who know me are laughing.) I have been a principal at two different campuses in the same district. The district is a large, suburban district in Texas with about 60,000 students, more than 40 elementary schools, 13 middle schools, and seven high schools.

Each time I was named principal, I replaced the same person – that hardly ever happens. Each time Dr. Justin Oxley received a promotion, I followed behind him. The first time, I followed him into Bradley Middle School, and the second, into Winston Churchill High School. The second time, I knew what I was inheriting and what he stood for as a leader. I knew the man, his high standards, and what he valued. This made the second transition more manageable and my situation uncommon.

For those of you who do not have the same luxury as I did, take time to fully realize and comprehend who you are replacing as a leader on your campus. It is crucial to consider the following:

- Did the staff love the principal or assistant principal you are replacing?
- Was this leader positive? Negative? Uplifting? Sarcastic?

- How did the community and student body view your predecessor?
- What traits made this leader stand out?
- What were things the staff disliked?
- Was the previous leader always in their office?
- Did the previous administrator honor campus traditions?
- What did the previous administrator focus on as a priority? What did they not address?

Understanding these questions can help you understand the culture of the campus.

I will share a common pitfall of first-year administrators that I want you to avoid. As you learn about your campus and who you replaced, you will be tempted to immediately respond to criticism of your predecessor. Anything you say about your predecessor will be immediately shared with them. As you learn who you are replacing, keep your critiques and criticisms to yourself.

Keep in mind that you can't be the person you are replacing. You were not hired to be that person. You were hired to take the organization to another level. Successful leaders realize this. They understand who they are replacing, but they are not a clone of them.

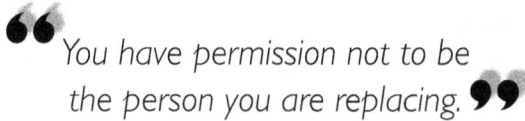

"You have permission not to be the person you are replacing."

When I was named principal of Churchill High School, a former colleague of mine, Mrs. Brenda Cerroni, was named principal of the middle school I left. As she learned about me as a leader, the good and the bad, she had to form her leadership style based on who she was. She couldn't be me, and I don't think she would want to be me.

As a new administrator, you must know who you are replacing. Once you discover who the person was, take what the individual did well and blend it with who you are as a leader.

2. BE THE HOPE THAT YOUR SCHOOL NEEDS AND DESERVES

With change comes great opportunities and great hope. For whatever reason, an opening was created on your campus for you to fill. You were chosen. Many applied, few received interviews, and you were selected!

With every opportunity we have to interact with the staff, student body, and community, it is our job to inspire and communicate the hope we bring to the job. We must clearly articulate our primary focus of leading a safe campus filled with optimism, hope, and joy.

A building administrator is as close to being a superhero as there is. I don't say that lightly. American Heritage describes a superhero as "a type of heroic stock character, usually possessing supernatural or superhuman powers, who is dedicated to fighting the evil of the universe, protecting the public, and usually battling supervillains." You could replace the word superhero with the word teacher or administrator. Don't we dedicate our careers to fighting evil and protecting the school from villains? (You could substitute testing and lack of funding for the word villains.) We don't wear a cape or a mask, but we are superheroes. We might wear suits, ties, or in the case of the skateboarding, tattooed principal in Virginia, Hamish Brewer, a ballcap. Our job is to inspire hope and be there when families or communities need us the most. Our job is to be a champion for teachers, to be the leader that the community needs, and uplift students.

When I was named principal at Churchill High School at the end of the first semester in 2018, one of my focus areas was to inspire hope and pride in our school. Not that those things weren't there, but I was going to ensure I was a little louder about how I championed the school. Every interaction with my stakeholders revolved around a slogan I developed #chasingchampionships. We would do everything to pursue excellence, both academic and athletic.

The following year, I utilized #defendthebrand and #bettertogether, along with #chasingchampionships. My campus athletic coordinator and head football coach used #chargeforward and #chargetogether. As our campus developed our core values and mission statement, I shared examples of students and staff living out these characteristics whenever possible.

When we are named campus administrators, we are anointed as beacons of hope who can change the trajectory of families, communities, and staff members. Let that sink in for a moment. We are not only the hope for students and families, but change also brings excellent opportunities for staff members. Sometimes, staff members become complacent (administration included), and change allows them to rekindle the fire inside them.

> *"We are anointed as a beacon of hope with the power to change the trajectory of families, communities, and staff members."*

Our job is to paint a picture of what the school will be under our leadership. I believe that when you speak about your school, your community wants their leader to be their biggest supporter and champion. Teachers don't want to hear our complaints about the job, the hours, or the stress! They don't deserve that, and quite frankly, many don't care.

We need to ensure that when named as a building administrator, we understand that we now have a place in the Hall of Justice, and the Hall doesn't allow any ordinary folks. Before you step foot on campus, ensure you fully understand the power your job holds for the hope of communities, staff, and the student body. The emphasis is magical; don't ever think it isn't.

3. YOU HAVE A MORAL OBLIGATION TO ADVOCATE FOR EVERY KID, EVERY DAY

At one point in her career, San Antonio-area Assistant Principal, Mrs. Tina Lozano, was accepted into a prestigious program of rising administrators. The Bexar County Prep Program is designed to expose future principals to various schools, management styles, thoughts, and opinions of educational leaders in South Texas as they prepare to become future principals. Mrs. Lozano returned from her first meeting with the renewed belief that "It is our moral obligation to advocate for every kid, every day."

While we all would agree with her statement, I want us to stop and look in the mirror for a second. Here is a quick reflection. Do we view our role as the building administrator as a moral obligation? Do we consider our line of work to be a calling to advocate for all students, regardless of their home zip code, irrespective of their hairstyle, or the bagginess of their pants? If I walked into any school and talked with administrative team members, they would all shake their heads and say, "All means all, and yes, that is our motto."

But is it?

For some students, we are all they have. We might be the last hope to prevent them from dropping out, prevent them from experimenting with drugs, or the only one who will help them fill out their FAFSA. Think of the enormity of the responsibility implied in moral obligation. The following examples represent real situations:

- I worked with a 7th-grade boy who said he skipped school in 5th and 6th-grade to get high with his brothers.
- I met with numerous 17-year-old freshmen with two credits who planned to drop out.
- Through a translator, I have met with families that risked everything to come to America, and their children didn't want to attend school. This broke the parent's hearts and mine as well.
- During the COVID pandemic, many of our students left school in March of 2020, and their families have given up on education.

If we view these situations as moral obligations, we will utilize every tool in our toolbelt to ensure a student is successful. We signed up for this job, to help ALL kids. If we consider our job morally imperative to advocate for all kids, we know what is expected. We can't give up on any kids.

I have had moments when I doubted kids and gave up on them. As I drove home from school, I swore that I was done with young Johnny or Suzie. But the next day was a new day and a new opportunity. Every day is a new day and a new opportunity. I believe in all kids; I know you do if you are reading this. How do we model this?

If we expect our teachers to greet every student entering their room, are we, as administrators, doing the same? Are we greeting students that we pass in the hallway or at lunch? Are we welcoming students to campus with a smile? Greeting the valedictorian, the starting quarterback, or the drum major is easy. But are we greeting all the students? Are we saying hello to the kid who just returned from a three-day suspension with the same enthusiasm? Are we saying hello to the students dressed in all black? Are we commenting on the student's new tattoo on their forearm? If all truly means all, how are we connecting with every kid on our campus?

Schools will never be the same after the tragedy in Uvalde, Texas in the spring of 2022. My biggest fear is a school shooting. I pray each morning before I walk onto my campus to keep us safe from harm. The incident brought safety measures to schools across campus. I am lucky that in 2015, our district dedicated funds to ensure that all campuses were fenced in from the public. Our high school has nine buildings, 30 acres, and over 150 exterior doors. We are entirely fenced in.

On the first day of school in August 2022, I stood in a full suit at the parent drop-off line and greeted each kid and parent. Later that week, a parent stopped me and thanked me for being out there, "You being there helps me feel safe sending my child to school."

I watched traffic flow in the morning, checked for dress code issues, and welcomed the students. I didn't think I was there to provide peace of mind to parents. I now start each day in the drop-off line. I don't have to check as many dress code issues, and I try to greet every student who enters campus with a kind word, a smile, and a fist bump. I wave hello to every parent and ensure everyone who sees me knows I am happy to be at work. I also give families peace of mind for the safety of their children.

When we sign up to help ALL kids, our job involves confronting educational practices that are not culturally relevant for all students. As the building principal, we must be prepared to shatter the "we have always done it this way" mindset.

The COVID-19 pandemic fully exposed outdated practices in education that need never to return! Being an advocate for all kids involves hiring teachers that match the demographics of our campus. I always believed, "You can't be what you can't see!" (Later, I will address hiring.) But when you advocate for all kids, your teaching staff's demographics should match the student body.

I hired the first female band director in school history. Ms. Amanda Stevenson is now a role model for all young ladies in her band who can one day see themselves as head band director. I hired the first African American head football coach in school history. Do children in your classrooms see themselves in their teachers? As an advocate for all kids, what are you doing to fill this void? Are you actively trying to recruit male teachers of color? Are we ready for this?

We can't be afraid to advocate for students whose parents have given up on them. Have you ever sat in a parent conference and listened to a parent scream at their child and use hurtful profanity directed toward them? After the conference, you see the embarrassment in their body language. You might be all they have left.

The student who makes your job complicated will attend tomorrow because the most challenging kids seem to have perfect attendance. (They will be on campus even if they are not in class.) You might be the only one who says anything positive to them throughout the day.

Sometimes, when I lay awake at night, the heaviness of my job sinks in. It sometimes cripples me. The weight of my community on my shoulders is overwhelming. I have often questioned my effectiveness.

As administrators, we have to forgive, forget, and move on. We can't take anything personally. Before you step on campus, you must understand that your moral obligation is to advocate for every student daily! If you can't wrap your mind around this, I highly suggest that you stop reading, and have a heart-to-heart with your conscience about whether or not this job is right for you. If you are ready for this challenge, then let's keep going! We have work to do!

Repeat after me: All means all.

4. THINK ABOUT HOW YOU WANT TO BE PERCEIVED BY YOUR STAFF, COMMUNITY, AND STUDENT BODY

It is imperative to think about how you want to be viewed by the staff, community, and students. John Hinds, a mentor and former principal in San Antonio, first mentioned this concept to me. As he transitioned from one elementary school to another, he spent considerable time thinking about how he wanted to be viewed by his school community. How did he want the staff to perceive him?

He thought about the following:

- What actions could he take so the staff could see him as positive and supportive?
- How could he maximize his calendar to be visible?
- How could he demonstrate to his staff that he was a lifelong learner?

He wanted to ensure that his words matched his actions. He thought about what actions could demonstrate this commitment to his community.

As a principal, I wanted the community to view me as an approachable leader. I wanted to be visible and seen. I considered this important. I needed to ensure that I built structures and systems to allow me to be seen in this light. It is essential to be strategic in accomplishing these goals.

Teachers want to see the principal every day. This reassures them. As a high school principal, I wanted to be insanely visible to the students and staff. I made it my goal to visit with every teacher every day. This became a challenge at a campus of over 2,500 students and almost 160 staff members, but it was important to me to be visible. While I do not meet this goal daily, it drives me to wander the campus and allows me to connect with students and staff. By challenging myself to visit every classroom daily, I modeled the importance of being visible to my leadership team.

I have always believed in the philosophy of people before paper. An administrator should only be in their office during the passing period when dealing with a crisis. During the day, our job was to connect with our school community. We could answer emails or prepare reports after the students and staff had gone for the day. My team knew that, and frequently, before the bell would ring, they were already in the hallways. If we expected teachers to be in the hallway during each passing period, surely administrators should do the same. This approach also goes with your numerous extracurricular events on campus.

At each school I led, I wanted parents to see my genuine enjoyment of their children's activities. If I was at a volleyball or basketball game, the parents loved that I sat on the bench with the team. I cheered the kids on and filled the water bottles for the team when needed. At one of the first high school swim meets I attended, the parents noticed that I high-fived the athletes and wished them luck at the meet. I spent time visiting with the kids and the coach and never realized that parents would watch my interactions with their children. But they are watching. And so are your central office leaders.

I brought sunflower seeds to the girls' softball games and sat in the dugout at baseball games. During football games, I poked my head into huddles, took photos, and celebrated with the students. As a former coach, this brought me joy and allowed me to build strong relationships with the athletes and coaches. Now, when I saw the starting shortstop of the softball team in the hallway, I could talk with her. This allowed me to connect with her and open the door for her to share anything with me.

I tell you this because it's important to consider how you want to be perceived by the community. Knowing that parents, staff, and students are watching, you need to be strategic in where you are 24/7. Parents can always find me complimenting the students with a kind word or a high five at the end of each concert and game. They could also see me helping stack chairs or assisting the directors with cleaning up routines.

When I transitioned to high school principal in January 2019, I created an introduction video that was shown to the student body. I wanted to make a strong introduction and connect with the community. I chose the theme "Chasing Championships" as the main idea of my message for the video. I wanted everyone to know I was here to support, champion, and defend our school. My Chasing Championships theme was easy to understand from a team standpoint, but I also discussed what chasing a championship meant behaviorally and academically. Everyone could understand the comparison and could relate to my expectations. Instead of listing a series of rules for high school kids that would be tuned out, the analogy was received well. This wasn't a spontaneous discussion but crafted in hours of quiet reflection. I wanted each student to know our school had high expectations and that we would never allow average to become acceptable.

Every Friday, I emailed the student body, sharing with them the thoughts that were on my mind regarding our campus. I shared challenges and examples of how students were living our core values. These emails helped craft our narrative.

San Antonio-area Principal Eric Wernli talks to his student body about the "Madison Way" throughout the year. This concept helps rally the student body by defining norms from hallway behavior to cleaning the cafeteria after lunch. The Madison Way helps set the tone for campus expectations.

Before you step foot on campus, it is essential that you genuinely plan out how you want your community to view you.

5. BRING THE NOISE OR DON'T BRING IT AT ALL

Every leadership book you read will tell you that the principal's tone sets the pulse of the campus. Someone once told me that everyone in the building caught a cold when the principal sneezed. That may not be a good saying after COVID, but we all get the idea. The principal's tone is critical to campus success. We owe it to our community, staff, and student body to bring our passion, excitement, and enthusiasm to the job.

As administrators, we are never allowed an "off" day. This doesn't mean we cannot take a day off. It means that when we are on campus, we must be on our game. I take enormous pride in having that extra pep in my step. If I don't have it one morning, it is my job to find it before the students and staff arrive on campus. Nobody should ever question if you love your job. It should be so obvious you could see it from the moon. Passion and excitement for our school, community, and job should never be delegated to someone else!

> "I wish someone told me it's okay to change the game, break the mold, and challenge the status quo. I spent the first six years of my administrative career doing what I thought an administrator did. I was miserable and felt as if I wasn't making a difference. This year has been a whirlwind of a difference! I am happier, my staff is happier, and our students and families are happier. To my fellow district administrators, it may seem that I'm not working since whenever they call my office phone during the day, I never answer due to being out in the building with my mobile office. I got more done this year by being out in the building! And I'm with the kids, which is the most important part of our role!"
>
> Michael Earnshaw
> Principal, Chicago, IL

Every principal should be their organization's face, their biggest supporter, and cheerleader. Every teacher and student should know when the principal is on campus and when they are off campus. YOU are the Chief Tone-Setter on the campus.

Coach Ralph RubalCalba is a prime example of a teacher who brought energy and excitement to every student he interacted with. He enthusiastically celebrated an offensive lineman with a pancake block and a young lady winning a scholarship for an art contest. His energy was contagious. Every campus needs people like Coach Ralph in its schools.

The principal should always celebrate and recognize students and staff. From morning announcements to staff and community emails, the principal should be the leader in positivity. I printed stickers that said, "Make Kindness Normal," and handed them out in the hall. I made bracelets that said, "I make a difference," and handed those out throughout the day. I greet every student and staff member that I pass in the hallway. While I don't know all the students' names, I make them think I do!

As an assistant principal, my colleague was Mrs. Julie Shore. She is now the Executive Director of Fine Arts for North East Independent School District. We celebrated teachers at every opportunity we could. If we found a bag of Lays Potato Chips at lunch (unopened, of course), we would take them to a teacher and announce that the teacher was recently named "Lays Sour Cream and Onion Potato Chip teacher of the day." The kids would clap, the teacher would smile, and we would go about our day looking for another way to celebrate someone. The teacher would get a bag of chips and a memorable moment to share with others. We looked to spread joy in our school!

San Antonio assistant principal, Ms. Jennifer Jones, utilizes the announcements to start the day with a smile. Anyone who listens to her in the morning can't help but smile as she celebrates student success by calling them by name over the announcements. She thanks teachers for attending games or concerts and incorporates a corny joke of the day. We often forget that kids are still kids. They like a corny joke or two.

Ms. Jones also plays music on Friday mornings at parent drop-off. She sings and dances and gets numerous smiles, and parents and students sing with her as they enter school.

I have often thought that schools and adults try to suck the life and fun out of education. This applies to the staff and students. The principal's job is to let everyone know how much they LOVE their job. Every educator wants an enthusiastic leader who supports their school community.

Dr. Lance Groppel believes setting the mood of the campus is essential. "Before school starts, walk the building and greet staff members." He continued, "Greet students and tell them how excited you are that they came to school today."

6. REALIZE EVERYTHING YOU DO IS DIFFERENT AND NEW
I have learned this the hard way.

Jimmy Casas, former principal and an inspiration to all administrators, often talks about his 20-plus-year career as an administrator. He jokes during his presentations that he would like to have his first 12 years back so he can do it again. Everyone who hears this laughs and thinks the same thing. If we could do it over again, we all would be better at our current job.

When you first step foot on your school's campus, you must understand that everything you do is new. The time you arrive on campus will be different; the tie you wear or don't wear is unique, and the way you smile or don't smile is new. The Adidas you wear on your feet vs the Cole Hahn dress shoes will be judged. Staff, students, and the community will notice everything.

San Antonio-area Principal Cynthia Rubio who has led three schools, believes that sometimes you have to go slow to go fast. "Results, improvement, mind shifts, relationships, and cultural changes take time."

As I laid out my vision for the new school year, teachers watched and listened to everything I said because they were waiting for what I would change. They also wanted to know if what I said matched my vision. Was I consistent?

My first year as a middle school principal differed significantly from my first year as a high school principal. I share here much of what I learned the hard way, hoping you won't have to experience the heartaches that I did.

I moved our faculty meetings from after school to before each month at my first school. Teachers would be more attentive before school, and the meeting would have an end point because teachers had a class during the first period. While over 90% voted at the end of the first year to keep this as the norm, a vocal group viewed this as a negative change.

As a middle school principal, I eliminated all morning duty stations and tutoring on Wednesday mornings. What does every educator need more of? Time! The idea was that teachers could get this extra collaborative time to work with their peers. Who wouldn't love less time on duty and extra planning time? I envisioned teachers reviewing lessons, data, and assessments in a professional learning community.

What was a win-win for the staff was viewed as a change. I also found that some staff members didn't know how to work collaboratively with their peers and didn't understand my expectations. This was a change, and I didn't communicate my reasoning for it well enough. It was received negatively because it was a change.

I implemented a staff book study during my first year. I loved to read, but I realized that not everyone shared that same passion for reading. The whispers started early: Why must we do a book study? Teachers quietly asked each other, "Is what we are doing not good enough for him?" The staff was not accustomed to the book study. I still remember a teacher coming to me with a copy of Dave Burgess's book, *Teach Like a Pirate*, in his hand. He said, "What will we learn from a pirate about teaching?" I hope Dave reads this and smiles.

On the contrary, when I moved to high school, a teacher approached me during my first few weeks there and asked me when we were starting a book study on our campus. They had a group that was ready for the book study. At the end of my first year, I had over 45 teachers participate in our summer book study.

At the end of the first faculty meeting, in front of my high school faculty, I said, "I know you are waiting for what I am going to change." I could see them sitting up in their chairs and paying attention. "The only change will be that you can wear jeans any day you want to school." The group cheered!

As I transitioned to the role of building principal, I was warned that in your first year, you should just sit back and observe. The only thing you should change is imperative to students' needs or the campus's safety. But I didn't know that everything I did would be viewed as totally changing the campus. While I do not regret implementing the book study or moving the faculty meetings, I wish I had fully understood how everything I did during those first thirty days would be viewed.

> "The final piece of culture that it is essential to remember as a principal is that EVERY SINGLE thing you do is under a microscope and will be examined against your belief statements to ensure that you are genuinely living those statements,"
>
> Dr. Lance Groppel,
> Deputy Superintendent of Administration
> Tyler ISD, Tyler, TX

During your first thirty days, it is imperative to truly grasp that everything you do is new and will be judged, analyzed, and discussed.

7. UNDERSTAND THE POWER OF THE TRIANGLE OF SUCCESS

In geometry, the most robust shape is the triangle. It has three equal sides, and all sides are needed to have a powerful configuration. If only two sides function, you just have a line, and a line can easily be broken.

The same triangle concept holds for our school. Three equal and vital parts determine our success:

- the students
- the staff
- the community

The triangle reminds us that all three components are needed for the success of the campus. All three have a voice. All three need to be recognized and acknowledged. All three parts are essential in the day-to-day functioning of the campus. The sides might not all have a vote, but they have a voice.

If the teachers and parents are happy, but the students are not, you will have an unsuccessful year. If the students and parents are delighted, but the teachers feel left out, you will have an unsuccessful year. (The last example was my first year as a middle school principal.) So, how do you get all three parts working in harmony? According to the Blueprint, this success comes from listening, asking questions, and discussing issues and concerns with all stakeholders.

I hired a new athletic coordinator/head football coach in 2024. We made the right choice, but it was not the most popular among my staff members because we did not select an internal candidate. We selected the right candidate for the future of our campus. Once my new coach stepped on campus, his energy and passion for the success of our student-athletes were contagious. Everyone realized why Coach Nate Shaw had been selected.

In leadership, doing the right thing and the easy thing often differ. I learned in this situation that doing the right thing, though difficult at times, is worth it. I told my administrative team: Happy kids, happy parents. Happy parents, happy principal. Happy principal, happy superintendent. This perfectly illustrates the Triangle of Success. As we begin our first thirty days on the job or the first thirty days of the new year, how do you plan on representing all three groups?

> *"The campus will not be named after you. It is not your school. The school belongs to the community. They have a say in what goes on."*
>
> *Dr. Lance Groppel*
> *Deputy Superintendent of Administration*
> *Tyler ISD, Tyler, TX*

How do you solicit students' voices?

Dr. Bobby Martinez, Assistant Superintendent of Secondary Education in Alvin, Texas, visited with his athletic teams and fine arts students during the school year when he was a campus principal.

He brought popsicles to these meetings and allowed the students to ask questions of the principal. He also made sure to thank the students for representing the school.

As I mentioned earlier, I would routinely bring sunflower seeds to the girl's softball games and visit with the girls in the dugout. They accepted me as part of their team, and I felt love when I entered the dugout. By bringing Dill Pickle or Taco Seasoned sunflower seeds, the kids let their guard down with me and saw me as an approachable principal who cared about them as individuals.

Some schools hold group meetings during the day, such as a student council or student government. These present fantastic opportunities for leaders to discover the truth about the campus.

While at high school, I had a lunch bunch that met quarterly. The counselors always picked students they felt would provide insight, which allowed me to meet some fantastic students I might have missed.

I caution you (as I laugh) that when you ask a student for an opinion, you have to be prepared for what they share. Kids are brutally honest. I asked, Evan, a high school senior about a class he was in. The teacher had changed, and we needed help providing the students with the necessary rigor. While we were working hard to provide for the students, I was failing them in landing a teacher.

"Can I be honest with you, Mr. Bloomer?"
"Sure. That is why I asked you."
"It's a shit show."

This was honest feedback from a young adult. Now, I could take his insight and do nothing with it or realize that this is his school as much as mine. We worked hard to ensure that the class and Evan had what they needed!

> *"When you ask a student for an opinion, you have to be prepared for what they share."*

I was covering a class when we were short substitutes one day, and I asked the class if anyone wanted to share anything with me. A brave girl raised her hand and shared that she didn't feel I supported girls' athletics as much as boys. She also believed my school's Instagram page (which I ran) was guilty of the same lack of support. This feedback was a punch to the gut but raw and honest. I attended events equally, but my beliefs meant nothing to this young lady because this was her reality. I promised to do better and did. I also thanked the young lady for her honesty. If you don't ask, you won't ever know.

When I became principal of Churchill High School, the school government and Parliament tweeted me and asked me to meet during the first few weeks to discuss their ideas for the school. I met with them and listened to their beliefs, suggestions, and concerns. Their energy energized me. I regularly begin the year by meeting with every club, sport, and organization. I share my big rocks (my most important work) with the students and allow the groups to talk directly with me. I seek their input and take their feedback.

When I hired a new band director at Churchill High School, I asked ten band students what characteristics they felt the next director needed. Their insight shaped my questioning.

Living in South Texas, we have beautiful weather five months a year and miserably hot weather the rest. On beautiful mornings, I sit on a red bench outside our attendance office, sip my coffee, and enjoy moments of peace. I can also talk with students and staff who pass by during this time. For me, sitting on the bench has two purposes.

It allows me peace and mental preparation for the day. It also allows me to be visible and get a pulse on the campus. I can monitor students in the hallway, with or without passes, and talk with teachers that walk by. I have had numerous meetings on the red bench. My head football coach knows to look for me on the red bench first before checking my office.

My interactions with the student body are crucial in building relationships, trust, and a bond with them. The word would also get out to their parents that the principal spent time with them and cared about them.

I also let it be known to any student that I was always available to visit with them at any point. They could schedule a time to see me in my office or visit informally at lunch or in the hallway. The critical part of this was that I was approachable and receptive to having a discussion about a matter that was important to a student.

How do you solicit a parent or parent's voice?
Just ask. I have hosted coffee chats with the principal. These were excellent opportunities to visit and seek input from family members. While I was a middle school principal, our Parent/Teacher Association (PTA) hosted an event where parents could meet the principal and the PTA president at a local coffee shop on the third Thursday of each month. We met during the day, didn't have an agenda, and were just there to meet with anyone who stopped by. At high school, each year begins with Bagels with Bloomer, an informal gathering of parents and me to discuss concerns, hopes, and our vision. Gary Comalander, a San Antonio-area administrator, hosts a Chat with Comalander throughout the year. This laid-back platform allows parents to meet and ask the principal questions that are important to them.

These are traditional approaches to seeking feedback. We are finding more and more schools reaching out to parents in non-traditional ways to solicit feedback from working parents. I make it a point to interact with parents at concerts or athletic events. I specifically ask, "How are things going?" Then, I prepare myself to hear how things are going.

During my transition from middle school to high school principal, I attended almost every event during the Spring semester. I sought out the parents that were in attendance. I made it a point to greet and acknowledge them and communicate to them that I was *there and I cared*. Sometimes, I would sit and visit with the families; sometimes, I would talk and move on. The point was that I made myself available if someone wanted to share a positive story or a concern.

I have also asked parents, "How are we doing?" I select the parents I know will give me honest feedback. During my tenure, we hired two new cheerleading coaches. Cheerleading in Texas... Well, let's just say they make Netflix shows about cheerleaders. I hired a former student and a family friend as a cheer coach. After high school, she danced at Baylor University in Waco, Texas. I wanted her to succeed more than anything. About six weeks after she started, I contacted a parent I had known for over a decade. She had two amazing kids and supported me. She wasn't afraid to speak, so I truly respected her. I texted her and asked how the new cheerleading coach was doing. Her response was, "We love Coach Jacques."

I was very pleased with her response, but I would have had to act if she had shared concerns. I asked. This is the only way to solicit honest feedback. You can either ask for feedback or bury your head in the sand and hope that what you are doing is working.

How do you solicit a teacher's voice?
I always identified students whose parents were educators. I made a point to reach out to these parents for feedback. They tend to be honest without causing issues and frequently will let you know of a concern before the general public does.

Stacy Kimbriel, a Dallas-area principal, attaches a link in all her emails that solicits feedback through a Google form.

Shane Mckay, a former principal in San Antonio, seeks parent input by having student leaders hand out iPads to parents at events and asking them to fill out surveys on the school's performance.
The teacher's voice is a critical component of the Triangle of Success. When campuses have a toxic culture, a lack of teacher input or a feeling of not being valued can be a prime cause. When a campus has a thriving culture, teachers feel that their voices matter and that they have input in the decisions made on campus.

During my first thirty days at a new job, I always made time to visit with every staff member. I took notes and listened to what was said. I wanted them to know that I remembered what it was like to be a classroom teacher. While principal of Bradley Middle School, I set up Popcorn with the Principal. I popped popcorn and made myself available to visit with teachers. In this informal meeting, I heard from teachers about their successes and concerns.

I have also always gained valuable insight by being out of the office. The principal being visible to the staff lends itself to being open. You can solve many issues and concerns with adults in hallway conversations.

My choir teacher told me a story about a colleague who illustrates the importance of visibility and seeking a voice. She told me he works at a large middle school and never sees his principal. She shared that she sees me multiple times a day, and we often have a conversation during these visits. I shudder to think about a campus without a visible principal. How do they seek the input of students and staff? I wonder what teachers say about their absence?

By fully embracing the Triangle of Success, you will have the blueprint to a successful administrative career.

8. BE INSANELY VISIBLE

Dr. Lance Groppel believes your first thirty days should be spent anywhere but your office. If you have to work in your office, plan on arriving earlier or staying later. But during business hours, you need to be *insanely visible*. Remember, you have the first thirty days to make a positive impression. While Central Office has announced you as the campus leader, the actual "interview" takes place with your community, faculty, and student body, who will give you their first impression. Each of these groups must accept you for you to be successful. How do you accomplish that? By being insanely visible!

I wear sneakers to work every day. I still hope that Adidas will give me a shoe deal, but until then, I wear sneakers because I try to log 15k steps at work each day. While it is physically impossible to be everywhere all the time, that is the mindset you need to have while you are a leader. Teachers want to see their leaders every day, students want to see their principal every day, and parents want to see the principal every day.

> *"I believe in a 'be at their door' policy! Staff do NOT have time to come to you during their break or conference period. Be known, be seen, be present. People equate how much you care with your presence. They don't know/ understand/care what you do behind the computer or desk. They know you value them if you are where they and the kids are."*
>
> Deanne Lee
> Former School Superintendent

Being insanely visible has another component to success. While present, it is so important to *be* present. Let me repeat that. It is essential to be present while being present. You can't just sit at a game and read emails on your phone.

At football games, it is essential to acknowledge and speak with the parents of the athletic booster club members, band, and cheer families. Dr. Bobby Martinez was also seen leading the student section in cheers while at a game. Not only do students appreciate that their principal has school pride, but parents and central office staff love to see the uniqueness of the principal.

> *"I also believe in There-and-Care leadership. In short, people have to see you there to know you care. I attend as many functions as possible and make it known to all that if it's important to you or our students, it's important to me. This involves prioritization, but I support all areas and programs,"*
>
> Dr. Bobby Martinez
> Assistant Superintendent of Secondary Education,
> Alvin, TX

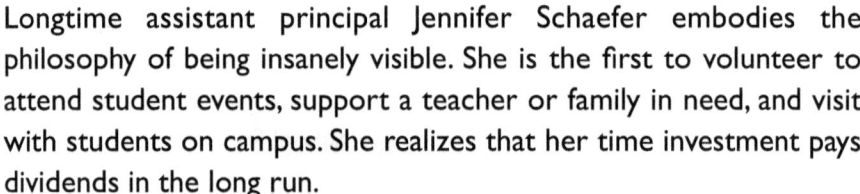

At every event we attend, a parent's pride and joy is doing what they love the most. We have the opportunity to celebrate with them!

Longtime assistant principal Jennifer Schaefer embodies the philosophy of being insanely visible. She is the first to volunteer to attend student events, support a teacher or family in need, and visit with students on campus. She realizes that her time investment pays dividends in the long run.

I bought a mobile desk during my second year as the principal. The portable desk allowed me to do my work in the hallway and be visible to staff and students. San Antonio-area Principal Jennifer Lomas utilizes her mobile desk to be visible to the students and staff throughout the day. She loads her portable desk with all that she will need to do her job from anywhere on campus. With laptops and iPads, you can work anywhere you can connect to the internet.

> *"Be out of your office more than in your office, and walk around the campus all day (minimum 2 out of 5 days a week). Pop into as many classrooms as possible to get a sense of what happens daily in your school."*
>
> Shane Mckay
> Former High School Principal,
> East Central ISD, San Antonio, TX

On my first day at my new high school job, I logged 18K steps. I slept well that evening. Being insanely visible allows your school community to get to know you, which is a cornerstone of success. Be visible, be present, and be excited about where you are.

9. YOU ARE A LEADER NOT A MANAGER

Much has been written and debated about these two roles within an organization. Both are extremely valuable and provide needed services. I would argue that you can't operate a school without both. But make no mistake about your role as the building principal. You are the leader of your campus and not a manager! Your assistant principals, counselors, and instructional leaders are all your managers. Both titles have extreme value, but both require different qualities.

Let's dive deeper.

As the leader of your campus, you are there to inspire the community, attack problems head-on, chart the vision of your campus, and serve as the face of the organization. Your charge is charting the course and leading the community to that destination.

As managers, you handle the day-to-day discipline, the nuts and bolts of working with students, staff, and parents, and ensuring the lights come on each morning. As managers, you put out fires, sometimes literally, and build strong relationships with students, staff, and parents.

As the leader, you will paint a vision that others will want to follow. You will hire the best people to help carry out your plan to move others out strategically.

As managers, you will ensure that buses are ordered for field trips, the calendar is up to date, work orders are entered, the cafeteria is supervised, and the teachers have keys to their rooms.

As a leader, you will rally the community around their neighborhood school, tackle issues within the community that bleed into the school, and offer hope for that zip code.

When I first became a campus principal, I worked in both worlds. While this is common, the campus leader must empower their managers to accomplish their tasks. Principals who work in the managerial world tend to get overwhelmed and struggle. When nobody is guiding the ship, the ship goes aground.
As I became more confident in myself and my leadership teams, I moved out of the manager role and settled into the leader's role. It was an important transition in my growth.

Alexander den Heijer, an author and motivational speaker, said, "When I talk to managers, I feel they're important. When I talk to leaders, I feel I'm important." A leader's role is to put their managers in positions where they can gain experience and become the next leader. As I stated, nothing truly prepares you to sit in your chair. That said, we need to put managers into positions where they can experience decision-making, processes, and the "big chair."

In the coaching world, great coaches often have "Coaching Trees" of coaches who once worked for them and now are head coaches or general managers. I view our job as developing our own "Principal Trees."

10. REALIZING WHO YOU CAN SHARE INFORMATION WITH HAS BEEN REDUCED DRASTICALLY

Think about this for a moment. Teachers have peers in the building to share concerns and struggles with. Assistant Principals have peers in the building. They can share dilemmas and frustrations they have with each other. Most schools have multiple counselors, instructional coaches, and even custodians who can confide in each other. Who does the building principal have as a building peer?

The answer is no one.

Few jobs in America are like the job of a building principal. The job can be lonely. The first thirty days are usually filled with the self-realization of happiness and optimism, but the reality is that it can be incredibly lonely. There will be times when you can't even share your concerns with your administrative team. It is imperative to build a professional learning network (PLN) for times like this. (I have devoted Chapter Two to this topic.) Every principal needs a coach. Just because you are named the principal doesn't mean you don't need mentorship, advice, and, every so often, a kick in the pants!

During her first year as an administrator, Ms. Jennifer Jones announced during a staff meeting that she had one friend on campus. Ms. Jones said that during your first year, you realize everyone looks at you differently. You are "one of them" and no longer "one of us." I discovered this very quickly during my first year as an administrator. I had a situation with a teacher and asked for input from one of the teacher's colleagues. Little did I know the teacher would be offended by this. I thought I was gathering information to have the whole picture, but that wasn't how my actions were interpreted. I was one of "them."

The job isn't easy. I warned you early on that it can be rewarding and humbling, often on the same day. Actor James Gandolfini played mob boss Tony Soprano on the TV show *The Sopranos*. Tony once uttered this chilling response to being in charge, "With all due respect, you got no ***** idea what it's like to be number one. Every decision you make affects every facet of every other ***** thing. It's almost too much to deal with. And in the end, you're completely alone with it all."

While being an administrator is not the same as being a ruthless crime boss, is his sentiment too far off? My first boss and mentor, John Mehlbrech, pulled me aside and told me that I quickly needed to understand who I could trust and share information with.

In 2015, I attended a week-long training at Harvard University. I attended again in 2019. (Yes, I tell people that I attended Harvard.) While at the training, I met a group of passionate and caring administrators whom I still keep in touch with today, and many are mentioned in *The Blueprint*. While I have always been a secondary administrator, I have received fantastic advice, suggestions, and fresh eyes on situations from elementary administrators. Mrs. Stacy Kimbriel, principal at McCall Elementary in the Dallas-area, has been an excellent sounding board and friend. You can follow her @skimbriel.

I would have never thought that the number of people I could share information with was limited once I became a principal. Still, I am thankful to the administrators in my Harvard cohort for this realization. The sooner you realize within the first thirty days that the circle of trust is small, the better you will be able to avoid the mistakes of many administrators who have come before you.

11. BE CAUTIOUS ABOUT THE ADVICE YOU ARE GIVEN

Crystal Romero-Muller refers to this time as being "... like shots in the arm of 'what?-they didn't tell me that part' every day."

You will have meeting after meeting with members from your Central Office administrative team who want to help you with your job and the head of the athletic booster group who wants to discuss their agenda and goals. As you get to know teachers and staff members, I encourage you to take every bit of information you receive with a grain of salt. While the intentions of parents, students, and teachers are genuine, sadly, some are not pure. Through the years, I have learned that not everyone can be trusted. Agendas and ulterior motives must be vetted when individuals give you advice, share gossip, or try to cozy up to you. I highly recommend Rick Jetter's *The Dunk Tank*. The entire book is written to help administrators avoid common mistakes. Dr. Jetter offers advice and suggestions in dealing with campus adults and provides insight into evaluating people.

I want to give you the magic formula for ignoring advice and direction. Making decisions based on your interactions, judgment, and gut feelings is essential during your first thirty days. Doing this will help you avoid getting trapped by lousy advice.

12. DON'T OVER PROMISE – THINK BEFORE YOU SAY YES – IT'S OK TO SAY NO

I run at a high level from the time I wake up to when I lay my head on the pillow at night. I rarely sit in my office and enjoy mixing it up with the students and staff in the hallways. I am asked for things during these interactions with teachers, from leaving early to more complicated issues. These more complex issues have often put me in precarious situations.

During your first thirty days, teachers will ask for many things. I caution you to consider what you promise during these casual conversations. I have learned it is OK to say, "Can I get back to you on that?" I have also learned that it is acceptable to say no. These two phrases can keep you out of trouble. The last thing you want to do in your first thirty days is over promise and fail to deliver.

I like to please everyone, and getting off on the right foot is extremely important to me. We all want to be viewed as administrators who can get things done, but we also want to be people of our word. We never want to promise something that can't be delivered. You can ask your leadership team for their advice by asking for time before giving a response. They can explain the context of the request and provide clarification and insight into the situation.

As we talk about how you build trust during your tenure as a leader, remember that your word is your bond. If you say you can do something or say yes to something, your staff members will hold you to that. Having to backtrack on your word puts you in a difficult spot.

I have also learned that the building principal must be able to say NO. I say it all the time now. If I don't want to do something, I say no. That doesn't mean it won't get done, but it might not get done by me. Saying no and delegating a task to an assistant principal frees you up to focus on other charges and builds your team's capacity.

During your first thirty days as an administrator, you must learn to listen, process requests, and become a person of your word.

PART TWO

The following items are actions and recommendations on tasks to accomplish in the first thirty days.

13. LISTEN, LISTEN, THEN LISTEN SOME MORE

I tweeted as I transitioned from middle school to high school principal. I asked my Professional Learning Family (PLF) to advise me on starting a new job during the second semester. I loved watching the responses stream in. Do you know what they all revolved around?

- Listening and visiting with every teacher
- Spending time with your coaches and fine arts directors and listening to their hopes, desires, and goals
- Seeking out your irreplaceable teachers and listening to what they need to be successful
- Visiting your parent-teacher associations and listening to their concerns
- Seeking out parents at games and events
- Listening to your students

All the advice was referring to the Triangle of Success.

Walking down the hallway of each school I led, I listened to what I heard and didn't hear.

- Did I hear laughter?
- Did I listen to kids debating who was a better basketball player – James Harden or Kevin Durant?
- Did I hear the students say hello when I spoke to them?
- When I talked to teachers or staff members, what did they say?
- Were conversations short, or did they genuinely want to visit with the principal?
- When I asked the staff members for advice on what they needed, what themes resonated within the discussions?

- When I talked with the parents, what did I hear from them?

A successful principal will launch a listening tour of the campus and community. Sometimes, we just need to stop talking and listen.

14. CONSTANTLY ASK YOURSELF "WHY"

Former principal Shane Mckay analyzes everything on campus and asks, "Why do we do it that way? Why do students leave the cafeteria the way that they do? Why do we have this policy? What is the purpose of this .. ...?" This philosophy is not an approach to implementing change but a way to fully understand your campus's day-to-day operation. "Why are we doing this?" should be on your mind as you watch and observe. The reason the policy was put in place will become apparent over a few weeks or months. If not, then that could be discussed as a possible change.

> *"Take inventory of what works well and what needs tweaking. After relationships and trust are built, get committees together to help with the changes,"*
>
> *Michael Earnshaw*
> *Chicago-area Principal*

Over the course of the year, I would bring these questions to my leadership team. Preface the meeting with your intentions for the meeting. (You have been watching, and you are simply asking why). A mistake I made during my early principalship was not explaining to the staff that I like to ask *why*. The team mistook the questioning as my way of looking to change tradition or their business. This was never my intention. I just want to understand why we do what we do.

As you analyze how things are done on your campus, ask students to explain a policy. Their insight is often spot-on. Remember, it's their school, too. When seeking student input and listening to their advice, they might have the answer to your dilemma. We just need to hear.

I have found that explaining why to high school students has allowed for buy-in and compliance with young adults. Why can't we leave campus for lunch? Why can't we wear costumes to school on Halloween? Why can't we have food delivered to campus? "Because it's our policy," typically didn't solicit the buy-in that I wanted. But by taking a few moments to talk to a high school student about why a policy has been successful, even if the students didn't like my answer, they appreciated that I had taken the time to explain.

Also, ask your best teachers why we do things the way we do. Often, they can explain why, which helps you understand.

15. TAKE EVERY OPPORTUNITY TO COMMUNICATE YOUR WHY

Like an artist painting their masterpiece, over the first thirty days, you should seize every opportunity to communicate your why clearly. Your why is who you are as a leader, what you stand for, and what you believe in. These are your guiding principles and your North Star as campus leaders. Your why is something you would never compromise on and never settle on. It should be loud and clear when writing emails or speaking to groups. It should be your educational philosophy, core values, and vision for the school's future. Your why should help you win hearts and minds.

During my first year as a principal at the high school, I sent a typical weekly email to the faculty and staff. Every weekly email had positive and uplifting quotes, pictures, or stories. I wanted my team to feel supported, valued and appreciated for their hard work. I took photos of events from the week and received numerous compliments for the tone of the emails. I wanted everyone to know how much I loved my job and community and that I wanted everyone to feel the same way about my school.

Even now, I still start every Monday at 7:30 AM with a faculty meeting, sharing and detailing all that is great about our campus. I now share a different message with my new teachers every Monday at 8:30 AM. These messages help craft our narrative and provide clarity and guidance that week.

At every faculty meeting that semester, I asked a former Churchill Charger to return and speak to the staff about what working at our high school meant to them. At the first meeting, former principal Joe Reasons spoke for 10 minutes about why he still considered himself a Charger. The entire staff could sense his pride in his job and love for working at their school. Shouldn't your staff leave any meeting that you lead energized and excited about doing the work?

Every interaction, every smile, and every handwritten card is an opportunity to reinforce who you are as an administrator. Your staff shouldn't have to read your mind; your WHY should be communicated so frequently that everyone knows where you stand on any issue.

16. EMAIL AND INTRODUCE YOURSELF TO YOUR STAFF AND ASK FOR FEEDBACK ON CAMPUS TRADITIONS

This is one of my favorite practices when arriving on a new campus or starting a new year. While email sometimes lacks warmth, it allows every staff member to have a voice and offers an avenue for everyone to provide feedback. When I became principal of Bradley Middle School, I asked each teacher to share their favorite tradition on campus and why they loved working there. This activity gave me an idea of the traditions the teachers held near and dear on campus. I quickly learned that the December faculty meeting was a breakfast and that a teacher roasted the principal and other staff members who did "funny" things throughout the year. If I canceled or moved the meeting, I might as well not start my job as the building principal. As I read the emails from my staff, I found that the campus valued being a family and that they appreciated being treated like adults. This information was vital. Email gives everyone a voice.

> *"What current practices have positively impacted the school? What practices/items are obstacles to student/staff growth that need to be assessed for possible action? I also became familiar with activities, procedures, and ceremonies that are essential to the school culture and should not be changed (at least not in the first year). I couldn't cancel these festivities, rituals the school had participated in for over a decade. I would end by asking about their expectations of you as the new principal."*
>
> *Jennifer Gutierrez*
> *Executive Director of Elementary Curriculum and Instruction, Former Elementary Principal*

During the first thirty days, it is essential to seek staff input on the values and traditions they hold near and dear to their hearts.

17. FIND YOUR IRREPLACEABLES AND SPEND TIME WITH THEM

Everyone is replaceable; some just hurt more when they leave. While we all like to think that the school would crumble without us, we are all replaceable. Life will continue, kids will still show up on the first day, and food will be served in the cafeteria. Each campus has teachers whose leaving would hurt harder and longer than most. It is critical that you identify these irreplaceables and that you spend time with them during your first thirty days. By doing this, you build trust and show respect to teachers who have earned it.

When I was named principal, reputation alone allowed many irreplaceables to stand out. These were long-tenured teachers, coaches, or directors. I made sure that I listened to them and made time to visit them in their classrooms to speak with them. The irreplaceables are the heartbeat of your campus. They are the teachers that other staff members go to for advice or look to on how to react to new policies or new administrators. Throughout my tenure as an administrator, I have utilized my irreplaceables as the group I like to bounce ideas off before I roll them out to the staff. Often, when I needed feedback on a campus decision, I would sit in Mrs. Karin Montemayor's classroom, where she was our science department chair. Her insight and pulse on the campus made her an irreplaceable resource.

I also firmly believe that your new teachers need to be included in your list of irreplaceables. Retired administrator Mr. Joe Reasons believes all new teachers are as important as your veterans. He feels that new teachers tend to be idealistic and open to innovation. Many new teachers are open to coaching and feedback. Mr. Reasons always ends his discussions with principals with a warning: If you don't treat the new teachers as irreplaceables, "they could fall into the trap of the Negative Nancys."

When you spend time with your irreplaceables, you are also seeking input from the heartbeat of your campus. During these visits, I would note what was said and what was needed. Your irreplaceables are critical components in the Triangle of Success. Spend quality time with your irreplaceables during your first thirty days.

18. ASK TO MEET WITH YOUR PTA AND BOOSTER CLUB REPRESENTATIVES

The principal and PTA president must be in tune and on the same page. The very afternoon I was named principal of Bradley Middle School, I called my PTA president, Mrs. Jeanne Pope, and introduced myself. A few weeks later, I took the PTA Executive Board to lunch so they could get to know me and I could get to know them. This informal lunch was an excellent opportunity to lay out my hope for our working relationship. I wanted them to feel comfortable with me. I shared my cell number with the Executive Board members because I needed their support. I have continued this tradition every summer, which has been extremely enjoyable.

Many members of your PTA or booster clubs have full-time jobs. Volunteers often work long hours on your campus to benefit students and staff. These people balance and dedicate their time to your school because it is important to them. The campus administration and staff must respect and fully support the PTA. The PTA President can also serve as a critical voice from the school to the community. Rumors or social media posts frequently distort the truth of school events. I have always utilized my PTA President to help communicate accurate information.

Let's use this scenario: One night, a Facebook post fanning the flames of an incident that allegedly occurred on campus scares the community. Most of what is said needs to be validated. Parents pick up the phone and call or text the PTA President to ask about the validity of the rumors. While FERPA laws prevent us from sharing information about students with anyone but their parents, having a solid relationship with your PTA can help you in this situation. If your PTA President has accurate information, this allows them to dispel these rumors. I have repeatedly picked up the phone and reassured my PTA President not to believe outlandish stories.

At the time I wrote this, Mrs. Lisa Thompson was my PTA President at Churchill High School. She had my cell phone number, and we regularly checked-in. Our relationship needed to be strong and one of mutual respect. I called her because she had the pulse of the community, and she always shared any concerns with me.

At the high school level, many teams, fine arts, and athletic groups have parent organizations that work closely with the school. I attend many of these meetings to let them know how much I appreciate their time and their children's involvement. Cultivating these relationships with your parent-led organization during your first thirty days will help you have a successful tenure.

19. PERSONALLY VISIT WITH EVERY TEACHER ON CAMPUS

With change come great opportunities. This is especially true when a new administrator walks on campus. It is also an essential reminder for long-tenured administrators to always remember what it is to be a teacher.

I publicly tell people that I try to visit every teacher daily. I know that most days, I will fail at this endeavor, but this lofty goal pushes me out of my office daily and drives me to every part of the building. I have often taken a list of teachers on my campus and put a star next to every staff member with whom I haven't had a meaningful conversation in the last month or more. Hopefully, the list is short.

Every Monday, I block off my calendar to be in classrooms. I only set meetings if they are essential. I also want to check in with teachers to see how their weekend was. Mondays are usually my favorite day of the week.

Every teacher comes to work every day to do their best. I have never heard anyone tell me they come to work to be average or worse. Everyone strives to make a difference. Marty Silverman, an elementary school administrator in South Texas for almost thirty years, shares this advice with new administrators, "By the time you have started the job, you will have been told a bunch of stuff by a bunch of people. This is the time to see for yourself what the state of the campus is like."

The famous "trust but verify" advice is my best advice over the first thirty days. I encourage you to make your own decisions and judgments based on the merits of the individuals during that year. One of my administrative assistants, the unbelievably capable Mrs. Terri Moran, scheduled fifteen-minute meetings with teachers at the beginning and end of every year. While this tended to tie me to the office, listening to what staff members wanted to share with me was vital. Here are some sample questions that you can ask during these meetings.

- Why do you love working at this school?
- What advice would you give me to help make our year successful?
- What is one tradition or activity that cannot go away this year?
- What would you like to share regarding your goals or hopes this year?
- What is your favorite candy, snack or soft drink?

I take careful notes during each teacher's "interview" and look for emerging themes. I also listen a lot more than I talk and make notes about what topics make staff members light up when they talk about them. I ask the last question about their favorite candy or soda and file that information for another day. Rewarding a teacher for attending a concert after hours with their favorite candy bar or bottled soda is a nice treat. When it's personalized, it means even more. Meeting every teacher during your first thirty days can build strong relationships for your campus's backbone.

San Antonio-area Principal Eric Wernli has successfully implemented stand-up meetings with staff members to solicit feedback. He believes that by standing with the participants in the hallway, he can seek input more efficiently. Principal Wernli's philosophy is that these meetings should be shorter than faculty meetings and to the point. He uses the same set of questions, and the feedback has helped drive decision-making on his campus.

Dr. Lance Groppel works with principals in Tyler, Texas. He emphasizes the importance of meeting individually with teachers as he mentors the administrators.

> "To me, the most important thing a new principal needs to do is to meet with as many stakeholders as possible. I would start with the teachers, but I wouldn't exclude students (depending on age) and parents. With the staff, I think it is important to balance getting to know them and the campus and allowing them to get to know you."
>
> Dr. Lance Groppel
> Deputy Superintendent of Administration
> Tyler ISD, Tyler, TX

Dr. Groppel typically asks these four questions during this process:

- If I forget everything you say to me, what is the one thing you want me to know about you? (personally or professionally)
- What do we do well as a campus?
- What is an area where we as a campus need to improve?
- What do you want to know about me?

The last question is a great chance to share yourself with the staff. Don't show all your cards, but they must walk away knowing a genuine amount about you.

20. VISIT WITH YOUR COACHES AND FINE ARTS DIRECTORS

This advice goes hand in hand with making sure you spend time with your irreplaceables. As a former coach, I understand the hours coaches and directors put into their programs. They don't do it for the money but because they love what they do. Knowing your coaches and directors will pay dividends for a successful year.

Directors and coaches are often nervous when any leadership change occurs on campus. Questions frequently creep into their minds about the level of support their new principal will provide for their program. You must reassure them that you will support their programs equally and with everything you have! Over the first thirty days, our job is to let our coaches and directors know that we appreciate and acknowledge their dedication and time commitment. One of the best educators I have ever worked with was Mrs. Julie Post.

Mrs. Julie Post was the orchestra director at Bradley Middle School for over 25 years. As a middle school program director with over 250 students in orchestra, she built long-lasting relationships with families and students. She was the only middle school director to have a full-time assistant director in our district. This isn't luck because of her hard work and dedication to the fine arts community. Not only was she one of my directors, but she was irreplaceable. What she and her program did for our school was as important as our state test scores. Spending time with her was imperative to my success. If she needed something, I wanted to ensure she got it. If she was upset, I needed to fix it. If she was happy, so was I.

Visiting with your directors and coaches lets you communicate your goals and vision for the school year. If you think about it, Fine Arts Directors and Athletic Coaches will interact with a large percentage of your student body. When your coaches, directors, and students in these programs are on the same page, your school year will function more smoothly.

Life at school seems more manageable when the football team wins on Friday night and the students have something to clap for. I can't tell you why, but we all know it's true. I have communicated the following to my Coaches and Directors:

- Coaches and Directors are natural relationship builders and must continue bringing students into their programs. There is a direct correlation between student involvement and high student success. I want more students involved, and I expect coaches and directors to recruit, not actively turn away students.
- Coaches and Directors must be active in their students' discipline and academics. We should always have students succeed and be eligible if they are involved in extracurricular events.
- The coaches and directors are essential to campus culture and activities.
- Finally, I communicate that I am chasing championships as a leader and expect the same thing from them as Coaches and Directors. This might look different at various times throughout the season or year, but the bottom line is that we are here to chase down the dream. I tell them that we don't get up in the morning to be average but to be the best we can be.

As a high school assistant principal, I had an excellent relationship with my athletic coordinator, Coach Glenn Hill. He became a mentor and a friend to me through the years. Coach Hill taught me that he expected all of his coaches to do anything the administration needed. He also communicated that he wanted to assist in any discipline concerns with his athletes or coaches. This is key on any campus.

He made it known that he had high expectations for his coaches as classroom teachers. He wanted to know how they were doing and ensured they had time to attend meetings and actively participate as part of their team. They knew they would have to answer to him if they didn't. It is this strong relationship that I was able to form with Coach Hill that shaped my expectations for coaches.

When I became a high school principal, I had the same relationship with Athletic Director Ron Harris. He hired coaches and played an essential role in helping hire other key leaders on our campus. When I needed help, I knew Coach Harris had my back. Not only was he a vital component of the campus, but he also became a friend.

I hired Nate Shaw in the Spring of 2024 as our head football coach and athletic coordinator. He immediately focused on building upon the great work of the previous two coordinators. The entire campus immediately felt his energy. His attention to detail was evident. He breathed life into our campus and returned our high school to be the pride of Blanco Road.

These three amazing men modeled for me leadership styles that were supportive and empathic for our community. During your first thirty days, it is imperative that you spend time with your coaches and fine arts directors because they are invaluable resources for implementing your campus vision.

21. GET TO KNOW YOUR SECRETARIES, PARAPROFESSIONALS AND CUSTODIANS

Many leaders will tell you that your support staff is often the heartbeat of any campus. Spend your first thirty days getting to know these para-professionals. They are the unsung heroes of any campus. Many of our support staff choose to work at schools to be around their children or work in their community. Many sacrifice the lack of pay and balance that with the joy and satisfaction in the school's success. With secretaries, you can empower the group to do amazing things by getting to know their strengths.

During my tenure as principal of Bradley Middle School, I was lucky that my secretary, Mrs. Lili Vasquez, had been at our school for over thirty years. She knew the community, our high standards, and the campus traditions. She also knew who to call at the central office when we needed help. I would often say, "Lili, can you call your contact at the central office about..." Sadly, Lili passed away in the Spring of 2023. She was so loved and respected that she was immortalized by our district on our Wall of Heroes. I was blessed to work with many other administrative assistants who were highly educated individuals.

Every administrative assistant will have a basic job description, but many of them, when empowered, will do so much more. In fact, by asking your assistants' opinions, they can problem-solve and help you analyze situations from a different perspective.

When I was named principal of Churchill High School, my secretary became my right hand. Without her, I would not have been able to survive. She had skills beyond skills. Without Terri Moran, I would have floundered. She is the heartbeat of the campus, and everyone in the community knows that.

Many times, families that are waiting to visit with the principal are not in the best of moods. Oftentimes, they are experiencing a family crisis. Mrs. Moran ensured that all families were treated with dignity and respect while waiting for a meeting. It was very common that families noted her attention to detail and kind heart.

Your secretary is irreplaceable. My secretary is the first person that parents, students, and prospective teachers meet. I've seen her welcome guests as if they were celebrities and console individuals when they needed it. You cannot get past Mrs. Moran if you are upset and often leave her office by hugging her.

A great secretary is a game changer. I am blessed to have worked with two outstanding ladies. A strong administrative assistant ensures that you are successful. They manage your calendar, ensure you meet deadlines, and calm upset parents demanding your time. I take time each week to meet with my administrative assistant to ensure we are on the same page. This is time well spent and allows us to function as a team. You are missing out if you don't look at your administrative assistant as a leadership team member.

I feel the same about my custodial staff. While their job description includes ensuring the campus is clean, many custodians go above and beyond. I have witnessed my custodial staff assisting parents with finding event locations or helping students retrieve lost items. Most custodians take great pride in the appearance of their buildings. I also challenged my team and me to get to know the custodians by first and last name. Would you only call a teacher by their first name? I made it a point to visit every custodian on campus, and I challenge each of my staff members to do the same.

Our head custodian at Churchill is a wonderful woman named Norma Rubio, whom we refer to as Mrs. Rubio. I make it a point to visit her weekly. I also ensure that the custodial staff is accounted for when we purchase staff shirts or have a luncheon. Often, for very little pay, they will have as much, if not more, school pride than other certified staff members do. I have also found that asking for advice from the custodians could often answer my question or solve my dilemma. Your custodial staff also knows where everything is located on campus.

During your first thirty days, sit down and allow the administrative assistants and custodial staff an opportunity to get to know you. Take this time to get to know each of them, their strengths, and their goals for the year.

22. CLEAN UP YOUR SOCIAL MEDIA ACCOUNTS

The minute you are named the campus administrator, someone will Google you. Another teacher will search your Facebook page, Twitter account, or Instagram page. Your posts and pictures will be saved, screenshot, or shared with your new faculty.

"Did you see what they posted?"
"I guess they like to take pictures of their food and alcoholic beverages."
"Did you see the language in the post that they retweeted?"

Your personal life and social media account shouldn't always intersect. My wife knows that when we go out socially with other couples, I do not want to be in pictures with alcohol or tagged in photos that imply drinking. I also don't want anyone to think that I am an alcoholic and an image can be interpreted in many ways. You can imagine that as soon as a student finds a photo of you with a beer, it will become the latest meme on campus.

As you are working toward sitting in my chair, you should clean up your social media presence. This might be simply making your pages private or taking down photos of you during spring break. We wouldn't want any of these photos to fall into the hands of an angry parent, would we?

I had a student create a fake Instagram fan page pretending to be me. They took photos off my Twitter feed. Sadly, I had to spend a few hours deleting all the pictures of me on my account. Your digital footprint should represent who you are. Your new staff should be able to spend an hour assessing your position on issues.

As the battle raged in Texas revolving around vouchers and Educational Saving Accounts, I used my social media account to challenge and question our elected officials. I found that this was a slippery slope. It came down to this. Was my Twitter account my own, or was I representing myself on that account as the principal of my high school? While I love social media, it can land you in hot water if you are not careful.

If you were to look at my Twitter, or X, account, @bloomer_sa, you would find where my heart is. You would see my why. But you will also see posts about running, pretzels, and pizza! You can monitor my school's Instagram page – @peopleofwc – and know I am a community champion. With social media, my staff and community know who I am before meeting me.

If you are reading this and want to get into education or administration, please know that anything you tweet, snap, or post will always be there. Please clean up your social media accounts before you are announced in your new position.

23. STUDY CAMPUS DATA AND THE CAMPUS IMPROVEMENT PLAN

You have already studied the campus data of your new school. After the emotions settle and you have your first quiet moment sitting in your office, I suggest reviewing your campus data and improvement plan again.

Analyze the data holistically. Any new or veteran principal should ask the following questions:

- What data jumps out at you?
- What did your campus do well? You should note these celebrations.
- What areas need improvement?
- What do you need to focus your attention and time on?

It is vital to then review the data over a three- to five-year period. What trends do you notice? In what areas have you shown gains, or what places have regression? Make notes of these areas. Post this data in your office and your questions and observations near the data. Schedule a meeting with your leadership team to hear their interpretations of the data. Their input and suggestions based on data interpretation will be essential as you move into the school year.

It is also imperative that you study the campus improvement plan. This plan is a collaborative approach to meeting your campus's needs. It should align with your campus data and district initiatives. The improvement plan is fluid. It can be updated and changed, and it should look different from the beginning to the end of the year. Your staff developed this plan with input from their department. Work to understand their thought process and their collaboratively developed goals. During this meeting with the committee, you also stressed the importance of the campus improvement plan being fluid and one that will reflect the school's needs.

During your first thirty days, you must take time to digest your campus data fully. Your campus improvement plan must reflect the needs your data reveals.

Stuart "Stu" Guthrie was named principal of Barbara Bush Middle School in January 2019. This was his first principalship. I asked him to share his thoughts over his first thirty days. Here is what he had to say.

> The thing that stands out the most in my first 30 days is that my office is now the "last door in the hallway." Being the final decision isn't a surprise; I've been in schools practically my whole life, but I didn't fully understand how your decision as the principal is genuinely the final decision. Even when I was in a position in previous schools to make big decisions, somewhere in the back of my mind,

I knew I could either appeal to or perhaps get vetoed by the last door… and now I'm in it.

Having this role has sharpened my need to collaborate and created an urgency to tackle difficult situations. Your time is not your own, which is fine, but you can't afford to waste an opportunity to complete a task, finish a conversation, and of course, make a decision.

This is the best job I've ever had.

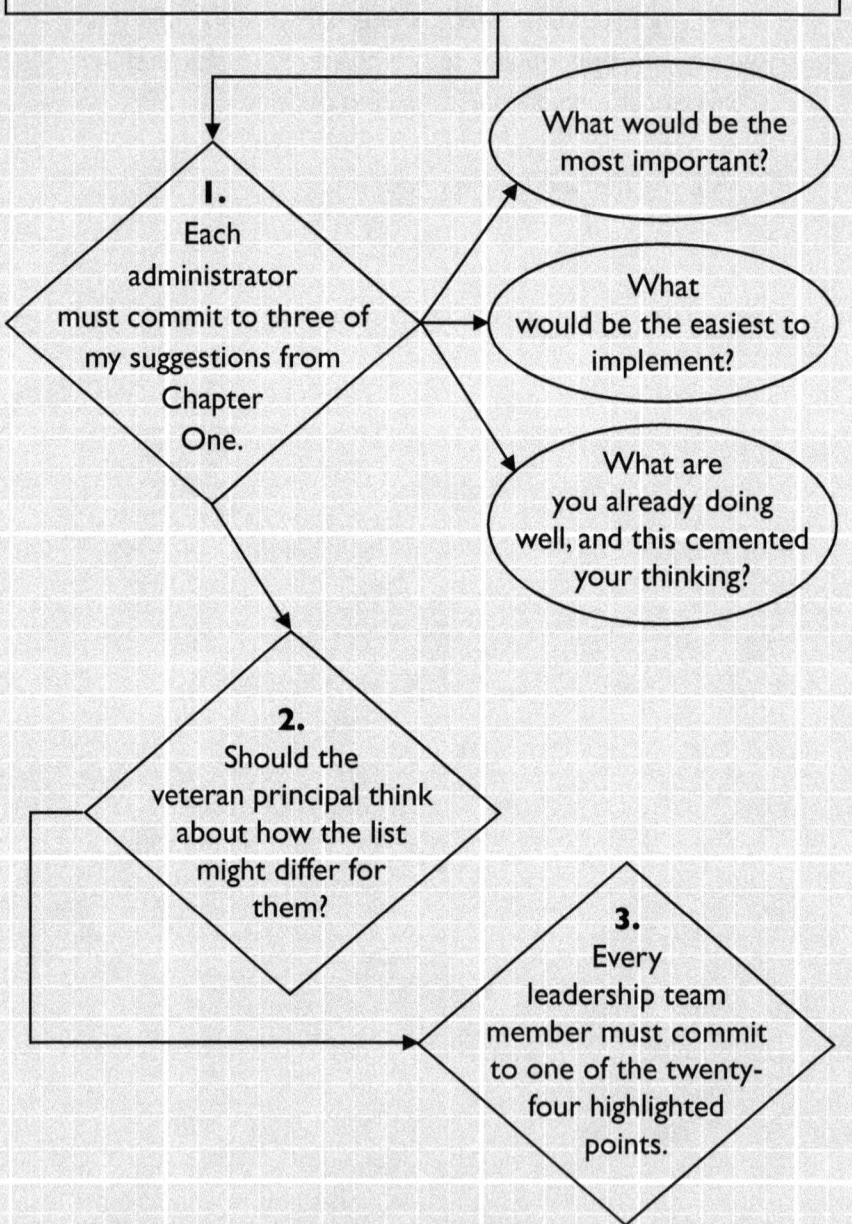

CHAPTER 2
Find Your Tribe of Mentors

As an elementary school student, I was fascinated by early Native American tribes. I learned how these groups banded together for protection, fellowship, and support. They traveled together, relied on each other, and survived because of each other. I studied them, and when playing with friends, we were always members of the mighty Iroquois Nation. As a building principal, I still believe in the power and strength of my tribe. Your tribe will be your secret to success during your principalship!

In the introduction, I declared that the job of an administrator is gratifying. Many weeks will fly by until you finally sit back in your chair to reflect. At that moment, you will realize with pride that *you are the campus principal.* A colleague, Mr. Pete Martinez, advised me to close my door, put my feet on my desk, and let the moment soak in. I was the principal.

But sometimes, the building principal is like an actor in a one-person play. The success of the play depends on the leading actor. The actor usually feels the pressure of the responsibility. The actor also gets credit for the win as well as the failures. While the experience brings joy, there are moments of loneliness at the same time.

> "Welcome to the Principalship and your first real taste of being lonely at the top; you need a strong peer group and mentor now more than ever."
>
> Crystal Romero-Mueller
> Administrator, Houston, TX

You must genuinely understand how lonely this job can be. I warn you that this job can take a toll on your health and family if you are not cautious. Administrators, if not careful, can gain weight, begin to lose their hair, and have their blood pressure skyrocket or worse.

> "The job is sometimes lonely. While you will have an administrative team to rely upon, it is so helpful to have peers who are doing exactly what you do and can understand your perspective. Sometimes, your admin team will be what you are up against, and you need trusted peers to bounce ideas off of and vent to occasionally."
>
> Stacy Kimbriel
> Elementary Principal, Plano, TX

Mrs. Kimbriel is precisely correct. All of us need a group. A tribe.

Suddenly, you can't share your concerns with just anyone. If you are not prepared for this, it can be disastrous. What if you faced a challenging situation as an administrator and sought advice? What if the advice you needed was regarding a leadership team member? Who would you reach out to for advice? The answer is your tribe.

Marty Silverman believes we will only succeed with a group to lean on.

> "We are a solitary bunch. We are usually the only ones on campus and function in isolation daily. When immersed in your campus, you lose sight of what is happening (think about people who can't smell the smell in their room because they are immune to it). It is important to have the vision to seek out and accept the mentorship relationship with another person who knows your job."

Shane Mckay echoes the same beliefs about the importance of having a tribe.

> "Mentors are there to sometimes just listen — as you move up in an organization, a leader's circle becomes tighter, and a strong mentor can be that person the leader can talk with regarding hopes, fears, and challenges."

Former Principal and current North East ISD Central Office Director Jennifer Gutierrez believes in finding a group to rely on.

> "The principalship is a tough job with so many imperative decisions being made daily. It is important to have a mentor(s) who has lived in those shoes to bounce ideas off. You need to have a mentor you can call on whom you know you can trust and who will be there for you without judging. Sometimes, it's a quick phone call about a procedure or policy you may not be familiar with. Other times, it may be a meeting to discuss an instructional practice or system you want to refine. Surround yourself with leaders who will ask you questions that will make you think and reflect on your current practice, leaders who will push you to want to be better daily."

Successful leaders realize that relying on a group shows strength, not weakness.

"You cannot go at it alone. Never will you succeed if you don't have someone with whom you can pick up the phone while in the parking lot when you need to get a 'for real' answer to a 'what would you do?' question in a tight situation on a short timeline. And you want to have those you can be yourself with and share what you 'really wanted to say,' how you processed situations, and ask for help. Yes, I said help. Being vulnerable is not a sign of weakness. It signifies a genuine desire to learn and grow from what can be shared or given.

Your mentor is not your 'last resort' call. They should be the first person you think of who you know has the knowledge and experience to help you slow down, think, and process. And sometimes, they're a good person to celebrate something you may think is not 'humble' to share with staff or parallel district colleagues."

Crystal Romero-Mueller
Administrator, Houston, TX

Ten years ago, a principal's tribe was traditionally only in their district or city. But with social media, a principal's tribe can now encompass the globe. It is this expansion of communication that allows educators to find their network.

To illustrate my point, I have never met Michael Earnshaw before. He is a Chicago-area elementary school principal. I connected with him on Twitter and liked a blog post that he shared. I started to connect more with him, and he joined a group of colleagues of mine.

Your tribe is powerful. I would not have had success as an administrator without my tribe. From my face-to-face tribe to my text message tribe, this mentorship has allowed me to grow as a leader. In Chapter One, I spoke about attending training at Harvard

University. During these training sessions, I met some of the most influential members of my tribe. Many of them are highlighted in my book.

When I applied for a high school principal job, my tribe prepared me for the interview. In fact, over the last five years, their group text has been some of the best professional development I have received. Think about that for a moment. Who would ever consider a group chat a relevant form of professional development?

The hope with this chapter is that you genuinely prioritize having a tribe of mentors you can rely on. You may be assigned a district mentor, and while this relationship is critical, I encourage you to seek out like-minded administrators who can serve as your unofficial mentors. While you might not need them instantly, trust me, they can provide insight, advice, and support. I speak from experience.

Some administrators have been swallowed up by the loneliness of this job. Like quicksand, loneliness and isolation can come out of nowhere. This is where your tribe of mentors comes in handy and frequently what keeps you sane. Mike Earnshaw sums up the importance of needing a tribe, "You need mentors because you don't know it all."

Here is my checklist for Finding your Tribe:

1. Your tribe won't let you fail.
2. Connect with your local leaders.
3. Utilize social media to build your tribe.
4. Realize that mentorship does not have to be face-to-face.
5. Never stop learning. Attend conferences, EdCamps, and workshops. Read articles and books.
6. Never stop asking, "What if...?

1. YOUR TRIBE WON'T LET YOU FALL OR FAIL

Anyone who knows me knows that I am not an adventurous guy. I'm not into extreme sports. I don't enjoy heights, so I don't enjoy activities that ask me to go thirty feet above the ground. However, many organizations today use team-building activities involving challenges or rope-based courses to unite. The idea is to build and inspire trust.

Project Adventure is a non-profit organization that utilizes rope-based courses to accomplish team building. I have experienced the rope courses twice while attending the Harvard Leadership Academy. Both times, the instructors pushed me out of my comfort zone, and I did things I didn't think I could do. Through teamwork, the Project Adventure group quickly helps you overcome all fears and brings your group together. The risk-taking and vulnerability required to climb 35 feet into the air are indeed one of a kind. Scaling a telephone pole and walking across a wire takes a total team effort. It takes a tribe.

The term *belay* refers to the team it takes to ensure that a climber does not fall. The group includes many individuals. In many ways, success as leaders is dependent on our belay teams. Before climbing the ladder to ascend the pole, climbers must ask the belay team if they are ready and if it is safe to begin climbing. Everyone then checks each other's equipment. Once the climbers start on this journey, the belay team's job is to encourage the climber and to provide precise & detailed instructions on their next moves to ensure they safely complete the task. The entire time, they are promoting the climber. Does this sound like what a strong tribe of mentors does for us?

Our tribe checks us for safety. They encourage us and give us specific instructions while we are on the "high wire" of the job. They keep us from falling and allow us to navigate our jobs successfully!

2. CONNECT WITH YOUR LOCAL LEADERS

I am blessed to work in a large district with fourteen middle and seven high schools. Since I have worked as a principal in our community's middle and high schools for over a decade, I have a bond with each sitting principal. While I respect all of them, certain administrators have become my go-to advisors for advice and support. It is these relationships that keep me sane and keep me from feeling the weight of the world on my shoulders. This is my local tribe.

In larger districts, finding those sitting in your chair is easier. Tracy Wernli, a former middle school principal at Northside ISD in San Antonio, sought out like-minded members of her tribe while gathering with district leaders. "I listen during principal meetings to what people say and gravitate towards those who think like me or have a school similar to mine. I avoid negative naysayers."

Bryan Norwood is a principal in San Antonio. His thought process and approach to leadership are contagious. Often, I will interrupt his workout at the gym to pick his brain about dilemmas. He also has the most impressive collection of sneakers, and his knowledge and love of late 1980s rap is energizing. Seeking out leaders like Bryan and listening when they speak are essential for all administrators. He is my EF Hutton. When he talks, I listen. (That might have been a reference that went over many reader's heads.)

> *"When at events that have other campus principals with schools of similar size and demographics, I make it a point to introduce myself and to connect, then follow up with an email to that person that includes my cell number. I reach out periodically to seek advice or guidance on how they've handled certain situations."*
>
> *Shane Mckay*
> *Former High School Principal,*
> *East Central ISD, San Antonio, TX*

As I have continued my principalship, some of my best mentors are principals at different levels within my district. Mr. John Hinds, a long-time administrator in my district, became my sounding board. While he was an elementary school administrator, his fire and passion for the job were qualities that I valued and wanted to replicate at the secondary level.

A key component of mentorship is seeking people you respect and value. Dr. Lance Groppel believes it is important to find mentors who listen. "I would also seek the counsel of those leaders that respond with more questions than answers. Those mentors focus more on your professional growth than telling you how they would do things."

If your district needs a strong collaborative network, start one. Seriously? Build a tribe? Yes!

If you do not have a tribe, you can reach out to those doing the same job as you and ask them if they want to meet for dinner one evening. San Antonio-area Assistant Principal Mrs. Tina Lozano helped organize a middle school principals cohort that met twice a year during the school year. At these meetings, she arranged for central office administrators to visit with the cohort and developed time for administrators to network and bond. This was integral to the cohort's success. Everyone needs time to ask questions and listen to their colleagues. It is within these discussions and networking that critical growth occurs.

What if you are in a small district with only one or two middle school principals or the only high school principal? How do you continue to network and grow with administrators locally who are doing the same job? Dr. Lee Vi Moses is a principal in Rogers ISD, a small district with only one high school of 280 students. He emphasizes the lack of different perspectives.

> "Since I am in a rural district and cannot bounce practices with other high school principals, I am constantly looking for ways to connect and share. Getting off campus with other principals is vital for developing skills to serve our schools. Holding to my commitment to collaboration in a small school, I must be off campus to better the school experience of a small school for my students. If collaboration has shown to be the right driver for teachers and instruction, then the same can be said for the principal. Because of that commitment to collaboration and movement away from competition, I have met some wonderful people who are so committed to their work; it caused me to take on a long-time dream of my own."
>
> Dr. Lee Vi Moses
> Principal, Rogers ISD

While I was an assistant principal at the high school level, I attended an administrators' cohort at Trinity University in San Antonio, Texas. This cohort met monthly and allowed administrators from San Antonio to meet and network. It also allowed smaller districts to provide their administrators with growth opportunities.

> "Being a principal is hard work. You need to have thick skin, and having a support system of people doing the same thing you are every day is vital. There is so much "assumed" knowledge that is expected. Help and advice from your colleagues and mentors will hopefully steer you in the right direction and answer questions about things you are expected to know, but no one ever told you or even gave you the manual."
>
> Mrs. Julie Shore
> Executive Director of Fine Arts, North East ISD

> "A mentor is also invaluable for navigating leadership's loneliness. This is primarily true in education where principals are promoted from working on a team of administrators to a position without an equal on campus."
>
> Mr. James Barton
> Superintendent, Caldwell ISD, TX

3. UTILIZE SOCIAL MEDIA TO BUILD YOUR TRIBE

What if I told you that you could have access to educational greats like Rick Wormeli, Todd Whitaker, or Jimmy Casas? What if I told you that he would respond if you tweeted Rick Wormeli? What if I told you Jimmy Casas would react to you on Voxer if you contacted him? How is this even possible?

I have connected with and met all of these individuals via social media. How would the average San Antonio, Texas principal, Todd Bloomer, connect with these educational greats? Ten years ago, the only way I would have connected with these experts would have been by attending a conference and getting lucky enough to visit them. Even if I attended a meeting, how much one-on-one time could I expect with them? I could email them or write them a letter and hope they respond.

LinkedIn, X, and other social media platforms have changed the game for administrators. Now, we are privy to their thoughts and mindset; they make it all available to us at any time.

> "It wasn't until 2018 that I discovered the power of Twitter. With Twitter, I have been able to connect with educators who have the same vision as myself. We're not tied to our offices; we know the importance of loving a child, not just teaching them. While many of my fellow administrators in my district do not hold the same

philosophies as me, I know I'm not alone in my rogue ways as my PLN is always a tweet away."

Michael Earnshaw
Principal, Chicago, IL

As an administrator, I have used Twitter, Instagram, and Facebook to promote my school. I hosted a book study and included the author. I used Twitter when doing presentations. I used Twitter when I needed to be reminded that I was on the right track. In essence, social media has become the chief of my tribe. If we flew a flag, it might be that of a bluebird or now a black X.

With all the awesome things I just described, some educational leaders do not utilize social media. How can we still have educational leaders not using social media to grow professionally? We are almost a quarter of the way into the 21st century, and educators claim they don't have time for social media. I have always found that we make time for what we want to make time for. If we're going to spend hours playing games on our iPads, we find time for that. If we're going to watch Dancing with the Stars, we make time for that. Social media should be viewed in this same light.

Participate in as many Twitter chats as possible during your tenure as principal. This allows you to find your tribe in the educators you connect with during those conversations. I have hosted chats and participated in them. They have Twitter chats for just about any group. I suggest that you lead your own Twitter chat on your campus. By modeling this, you allow others on your campus to find educators they can connect with and promote lifelong learning.

LinkedIn has become a platform I utilize to advertise job opportunities on campus. But it is so much more than that. The connections it provides for administrators are unbelievable.

When looking to expand your tribe, use social media as the primary agent to help build and secure your network.

4. MENTORSHIP DOES NOT HAVE TO BE FACE TO FACE

I consider noted authors Brian Buffini, Ryan Holliday, and Tom Byleau mentors, yet I have never met them. So, how can they be my mentors?

In our current time, mentorship isn't just face-to-face from people who know me. We live in an exciting time. The devices we carry in our pockets or wear as wristwatches are our cameras, computers, music players, and wallets. Through technology, I have been able to connect with leaders in a variety of fields. They don't know me, and I don't claim to know them, but they push my thinking and propel me forward.

I have utilized the leadership podcasts of Jimmy Casas, Dr. Brandon Beck, and Dr. Darrin Peppard to inspire and guide me in my work. These podcasts give me access to some of the brightest minds and most successful people in their fields. Their advice and suggestions are free to listen to, and I have found great value in sharing podcasts that push my thinking with members of my tribe.

I have also fallen back in love with reading as an adult. Reading became a stress reliever and also something I did for enjoyment. Reading is another relatively inexpensive way to be mentored. The authors of the books have become unseen members of my tribe.

I focus on leadership books and look for education-related books from different arenas. *Losing the Signal* is the story of the rise and fall of the Blackberry phone. On its own, it has nothing to do with my job as a school administrator. However, studying the parallels between the company's rise and fall and comparing it to public schools is eye-opening. Those who fail to change are left behind or are nonexistent.

According to blogger Jim Kwik, the average person reads two or three books yearly, and the average company's CEO reads four or five books monthly. Let that sink in for a minute. What leadership lesson can we learn from this? I have always found great value in studying successful leaders. Why wouldn't I follow suit if they have specific characteristics that allow them to succeed? I want to be in their tribe!

> " *The average person reads two or three books yearly, but the average CEO reads four or five books a month!* "

I have heard this statement many times before: Sit with winners; the conversation is different. If you know of a school or principal doing great things, why are you not reaching out and trying to connect with them? With email and social media, connecting is easy.

Seek out alternative approaches to mentorship, and be a lifelong learner to be successful in your profession. Your 21st-century tribe isn't just people that you know.

5. NEVER STOP LEARNING

Think of yourself as a detective throughout your first year on the job. You are searching for a tribe, a group that will nurture and support you. I use the detective analogy because you gather input and listen to your peers. When you find someone, reach out & join their tribe. With that said... nobody likes a freeloader. As I have encouraged you to find your tribe, I also emphasize the importance of feeding the tribe by actively pushing the group's thinking. Native

American tribes were initially formed with an unwritten agreement that everyone contributed. Jobs, decisions, and obligations were shared between the tribe members. Everyone pulled their weight. If you chose not to contribute, you could be removed from the tribe.

Our professional tribe works much the same way. Within our group, we are expected to contribute to others' needs, problem-solve, push the envelope, and support each other on the job. As I ascended the career ladder, my tribe became smaller. That doesn't seem right, does it? The social media accounts continued to rack up the number of followers, but my tribe dwindled because I became more selective about whom I let into my tribe.

As you mature in your leadership experiences, or the higher up the career ladder you climb, you may only surround yourself with those you feel can help you accelerate your thinking. Sometimes, you look and listen and lose patience with those you think are not "all in" or don't seem fully committed to making fundamental differences. If we view the pinnacle of our career as beginning the principalship, we will have a short job. We need our professional learning network to be there for us, but we also need to be able to provide support to others. We need to feed the group that gives to us.

In the spring of 2018, I sought something to jump-start my thinking. I wanted to create something that pushed the thinking of my tribe. Based on an idea from my colleague, John Hinds, I started a weekly email chain to my tribe. I called the chain -- *What gets me going!* At the time, I hoped that this would be what I needed.

I shared my thoughts and the books I was reading and asked my tribe to help with this effort I was mulling over. I started with principals and directors within my district. I asked them to ponder any issue and respond if it moved them. Like all new ideas or initiatives, it moved slowly. I received compliments but didn't get the traction I wanted with the discussion.

So, I removed those who were not contributing or reading the chain. Others asked to join, the conversation picked up, and the word got out. I was feeding the tribe, and the tribe was providing for me. I now blog once a week instead of using the email chain.

6. NEVER STOP ASKING, "WHAT IF?"

If you are careful with the selection of your tribe, the members will motivate you to be your best. Finding these like-minded individuals is critical to your development and growth. Will Rogers said it best, "Even if you are on the right track, you will get run over if you just sit there." Simply because you were named principal or an assistant principal doesn't mean you can stop learning or growing. The key to being a successful leader will depend on what you do after being promoted to leadership.

I conducted a book study with the athletic coaches at my middle school. I wanted to model for them continued growth and cultivate discussions on how our coaches could continue to improve. We read the book *Legacy* by James Kerr. The book highlighted the All Blacks, the most successful Rugby team from New Zealand. The book shared the characteristics and culture of the New York Yankees of Rugby.

One of their key traits, and possibly the reason they were successful year after year, is what they call *Go For the Gap*. They believe that the time to change happens when you are on top, not when you realize that you need to change. This concept can be challenging for educators to grasp as school leaders.

With continual planning being the key to success, I have expanded my long-term planning to 10, 15, 25, and 50 years later. By doing this, everything is on the table for what your school could or should look like. The discussions are fascinating as you are trying to predict what life will be like when you might have passed from this earth. It is during these brainstorming sessions the next big idea is born.

Once born, the next step is laying the groundwork to get there. I call this process Education 2050.

Hockey great Wayne Gretzky was asked how he maintained his success year after year. He said, "I don't skate to where the puck is. I skate to where the puck is going to be." Like Gretzky, Hamish Brewer, the tattooed, skateboarding principal, is constantly planning. He talks about being relentless regarding your job and your learning. As connected principals, we need to realize that growth is necessary to stay caught up and succeed for those who need us the most: our school community.

My trip to California to tour leading tech companies speaks to this belief and philosophy. Top executives at organizations like Google, Apple, or Airbnb have a mindset of constant questioning. Their approach to problems or areas of concern is one that educators should emulate.

Here is Google's approach to problems:
  If users can't spell, it's our problem.
  If they don't know how to form the query, it's our problem.
  If they don't know what words to use, it's our problem.
  If they can't speak the language, it's our problem.
  If there's not enough content on the web, it's our problem.
  If the web is too slow, it's our problem.
  We look at the whole issue.

Take this in for a moment.
  Is this your approach to educating students on your campus?
  If the student can't spell, whose problem is it?
  If a student can't pass a standardized test to fulfill their goals for the future, whose problem is it?

Do you see my point? Your tribe will push your thinking and support you as you navigate the principalship and continue to ask, "What if?"

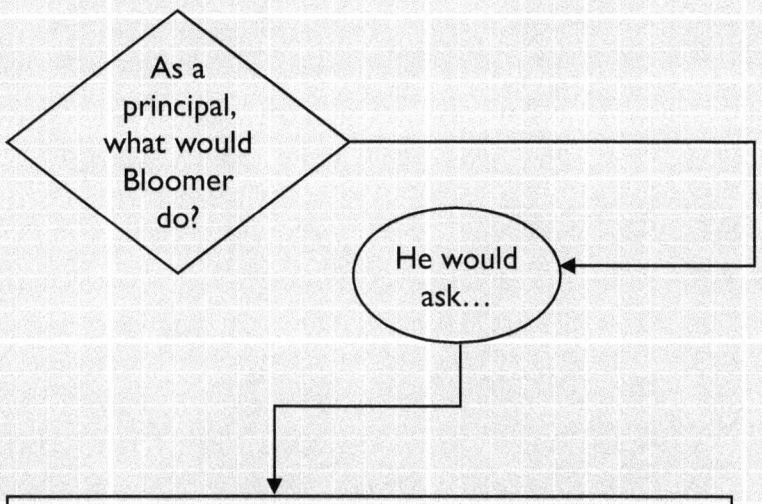

- Are you honestly searching, recruiting, and growing your tribe of leaders?
- How can we connect with leaders outside the educational family to help us grow as leaders?
- How are you, as the campus leader, providing opportunities for your staff to continue to grow?

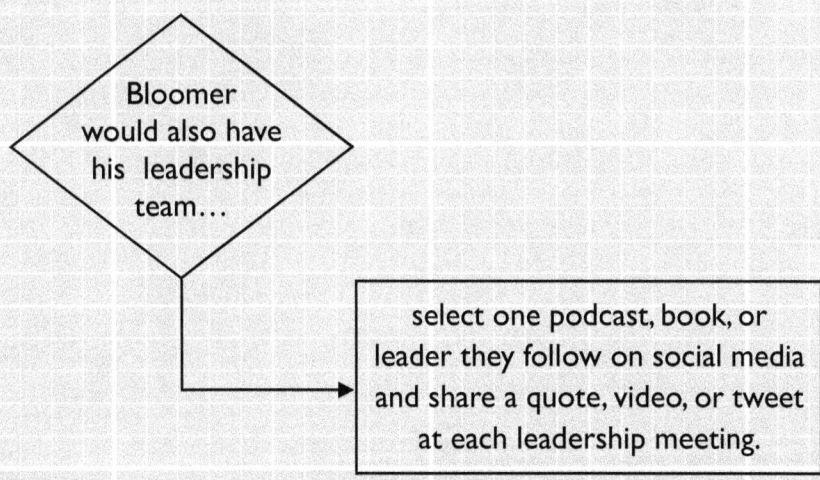

CHAPTER 3
Establishing, Shaping, and Managing Campus Culture

Be your biggest cheerleader! Be a champion of your school. Leverage social media to give your families a glimpse into the campus. Use this tool to your advantage to share your core beliefs, who you are as a leader, and the successes of students and staff at your campus. Take pictures of those moments that tell the story of truths shining from smiling students' faces, engaged and committed teachers, and your parents on campus being a genuine part of the school community.

Every administrator will tell you that shaping campus culture is one of the most critical aspects of our work. We all can recite quotes about how culture eats everything else for breakfast. But, do you know how to shape the culture you desire on campus? Is there a formula, or is your plan to use "a hope and prayer" approach?

Did they teach you how to develop a strong campus culture in "principal school?" If they did, I missed that class. If you are like me, you might need to learn what school culture is. Successful administrators follow a tried-and-true formula to shape campus culture. The inexperienced or poor administrators wing it. I was winging it during my first year. Culture is never something that can be left to chance. Culture must be worked on, nurtured, and fed daily like a garden. Strong leadership matters when shaping school culture! A strong culture can be eroded and destroyed overnight, and a poor culture can be rebuilt relatively quickly.

Sporting teams provide beautiful examples of both successful and unsuccessful cultures. The New York Knicks of the National Basketball Association (NBA) was once a pride-filled organization. I looked up to players like Bernard King and Patrick Ewing. The team played in, but lost, the NBA championships in 1994 and 1999. Since then, the team has fallen on hard times.

In 1999, team president and owner James Dolan was given more team control. (I point this out to illustrate my point about culture and how one person can influence it.) Fast forward twenty years. The Knicks have yet to return to the NBA Finals; they have only had one winning season since then and only made the playoffs twice (both first-round losses). Fans and players blame the owner.

I don't know the man, but I am sure he is a wonderful person who cares a lot about the Knicks. However, during the free-agent frenzy in the summer of 2019, the Knicks failed to sign any big-name free agents despite having tons of money. Current NBA player Patrick Beverly was on the ESPN show *The Jump* when asked about the Knicks' chances in free agency to attract any stars. Beverly indicated that the Knicks' culture needed to change and blamed the owner, James Dolan. He even went so far as to say that Dolan needed to sell the team. Beverly describes how one person's actions can negatively affect an organization's culture. I share this story because campus culture is delicate and should be treated like the golden ticket to your principalship.

Fast-forward again to 2024, and the Knicks have returned to legitimacy. How? They hired the right people and developed a plan to bring them glory. They were steadfast in their approach and didn't waiver from their vision, which has made the Knicks cool again.

But I must admit, I was one of those administrators who didn't know how to implement, maintain, build upon, or create the campus culture I wanted when I first sat in the big chair in 2014. I assumed that I could do it just by being me. Boy, was I wrong.

Culture is your campus's shared values, norms, beliefs, and actions. I was naive and believed that culture was providing perks to my staff, like a jeans pass, fruit-infused water, or organizing happy hours. With these actions, the school would function smoothly, right?

As I grew as an administrator, it became apparent that culture was the school's belief system, core values, vision, norms, and what we wanted our school to be known for. The free coffee, jeans pass, and snacks were the perks of working on my campus. I believe that the key to shaping campus culture is clearly and articulately communicating your vision.

I love to talk about my campus. Nothing gets me more excited than talking about how extraordinary my campus is. I feel an adrenaline rush when I brag about all the unique and special things that make my school the best in South Texas. I have a thirty-second elevator speech ready to go at all times about my school and why my high school is the only place for a family. If you can't stop on a dime and deliver an elevator speech about your campus, I highly recommend you create one.

One significant component of building a culture is to have you, the principal, be the biggest cheerleader on campus. You are the face of the organization. You have to lead the celebrations of your staff! I am going to celebrate student and staff success at every opportunity. I will be the school's champion and the defender of my community. I am going to tell our story before someone else does.

I routinely use social media to help create what I want our school to be known for. I utilized #chasingchampionship to tweet excitement about the staff I was hiring, the momentum our school was gaining based on the hires, and the team learning and growing over the summer. I wanted to control my message and help create what I wanted my school to be known for.

> "I ensure that every staff member has my own personal philosophy and vision statement in their hands. In addition, I encourage my new hires to read my blog (which outlines many of my stances on various subjects) and follow me on Twitter to get a flavor of my educational preferences and priorities."
>
> Stacy Kimbriel
> Elementary Principal, Plano, TX

On any campus where I am the principal, we live these core values: Family, Innovation, Positivity, Trust, and Collaboration. I weave these core values into every conversation, email, and meeting. I also hang signs around campus that speak to our culture. I ensure the campus displays student artwork, student projects, and motivational slogans.

Our campus created shared norms:
We Care – We Create – We Compete
You must ask yourself, do your values, norms, and beliefs match your actions? Are all of your actions and interactions aligned with your core values? If not, your campus culture will suffer.

Another component to a strong campus culture revolves around supporting the teachers in your building. In Chapter One, I stressed the importance of building relationships with your constituents. As you build these relationships, you will be able to listen to your staff's needs and be able to help and support them.

I have often said that if you show me a campus with a strong culture, I will point to a campus with a strong system for teachers to share their needs with the administration. The opposite is also true. If a campus lacks the mechanisms for teachers to feel valued and supported, I will show you a school with a poor campus culture.

Now, I will be the first to admit that I am not infallible on being a principal. I have failed many times during my tenure, but I have learned from these failures and have something to share about campus culture. I call this section of the book A Tale of Two Principalships.

I have been blessed to serve as the principal of two schools, and my time at Bradley Middle School has made me a better administrator at my current school. The next part is difficult to share and hard to write, but *The Blueprint* needs to provide you with the pitfalls and lessons learned about how campus culture can slip through your fingers in minutes. Even so this story is also one of redemption.

As I transitioned to my current role as a high school principal, I reflected on the mistakes I made during my first tenure as a building principal. I did not want to dig myself into the same hole I put myself in my first year. I reread my blueprint to ensure I got everything as I moved to my new role. I had an opportunity to redo it. Not many of us get that!

When I was growing up, every show I watched seemed to have quicksand traps around every corner. Do you remember quicksand? It was a genuine fear of mine. I honestly felt like outside of my neighborhood, if I weren't careful, I would fall into quicksand and possibly die.

While I never fell into quicksand as a kid growing up in New York, I fell into it during my first year on the job as a principal. Going into my principalship, I knew to keep everything the same. I knew my job was to build relationships and connect with the community. The school was in good shape; I just needed to continue to guide it forward. I knew my mission, yet I fell into quicksand.

When I arrived on campus, I inherited an excellent, veteran staff of caring adults. Many teachers had been there for their entire careers. They had watched each other's children grow up, and they had become their own tight-knit family. When I asked my staff members what they loved about the campus, they cited being a family as their number one draw.

Many systems and structures I discuss in Chapter One were developed and implemented after my first year. As you read more, you will understand.

As I joined the school community, the makeup of the campus was drastically changing. The demographics mirrored the city of San Antonio. The school was about 40% economically disadvantaged, up from 8% in 2007. The school had an outstanding reputation for academic success.

My twin daughters were students at my middle school while I was the principal. They loved their teachers. They would hang out in their teachers' rooms before and after school. My daughter, Tori, and her friends even had a Thanksgiving lunch with her favorite teacher, Stefanie Gorner, during her lunch period. What teacher gives up their 30-minute lunch to eat with kids? The teachers at Bradley Middle School did.

But if I am honest, my first year was miserable. I was stuck in the quicksand and sometimes wished I would have just been swallowed up. The state test scores were good, not excellent, but the community was happy, and the student body was well-behaved. With a tweak here or there, the school had the potential to be the best in the city. My approach to the "tweak here or there" was met with resistance. I had many people who were kind and friendly to me.

Still, I was an outsider, and everything about me was different -- I was into social media, I was unorthodox, I was loud, I was constantly somewhere, and I always asked why.

Reflecting on my first year, I realized that my vision for the campus was the same as that of the teachers. I wanted our school to be the best in the city. I just failed to articulate that vision clearly and consistently. This was all my fault.

As a leader, I take great pride in my communication. I am upfront, an open book, and proactive. But my lack of clear communication was my quicksand. As I got to know my building, staff, and school during my first year, I spent much time in classrooms and hallways trying to be visible and getting to know my staff. While visiting classrooms, I shared with the staff all the outstanding teaching that was going on. I wanted to celebrate it! I wanted the team to know I appreciated their hard work and the experiences they created for students. I shared these success stories via email, social media, or staff meetings. I told colleagues about the great things that their peers were doing.

However, only some staff members appreciated that I was in classrooms as much as I was. Since I celebrated the fantastic experiences I encountered, I also started questioning the sub-par classroom experiences I saw. When I began to see teacher-centered lessons rather than student-centered, I questioned why. As other colleagues implemented high levels of student engagement activities, I pushed teachers to strive for greatness. I suggested strategies that helped raise engagement. I encouraged "Turn and Talks" and reflection questions to ensure students were engaged. I also offered to connect teachers with others who successfully implemented these best practices, thinking I was assisting teachers.

The test scores were solid at Bradley. But I viewed the principalship as: *What have you done for me lately?* Nothing was guaranteed on state assessment each year. And remember, I was chasing championships. I wasn't in the market for anything other than the best; our kids deserved that.

I failed to realize that the staff would circle the wagons when one of them was being questioned. The conversation in the lunch room was about me rather than how I wanted it to be. Most of them probably realized "Old Bob" was a poor teacher, but they had known him for twenty years.

"Why is he doing this to Bob? Wasn't this good enough in years past?"

One teacher said, "Weren't we just named a Blue Ribbon School five years ago?"

Now, let's pause for a moment.
At the time I wrote this, I utilized video at Churchill High School to help teachers grow. I recorded pieces of lessons and sharethem with staff members. We followed up a few days later and discussed what they took away from their video. *I was able to do this because of the trust I had built with the staff.* The culture on my campus was one of personal growth. I was also seen as a resource rather than just an administrator who entered classrooms a few times yearly because they had to. What I learned from my first year at Bradley has allowed us to create a campus culture that supports this.

Now, back to my first year at Bradley.

I was struggling and doubting myself. I thought I was helping, but everything I did was failing. I allowed misinformation about my intentions to fill in the gaps by failing to communicate why I was challenging instructional practices.

They said, "He is trying to get rid of people." "He wants to bring in his people."

Again, I should have stopped and explained to the staff that I am naturally curious. I wanted what every teacher wanted: for our campus to continue to be recognized for its greatness. Looking back, I should have stopped and explained my rationale to the campus. If I had done this, I could have saved some hard feelings. Instead, I kept trying to dig myself out of the quicksand. Another slip-up on my part was not censoring my thoughts.

For example, I was meeting with a teacher in the first year, and I could tell she was nervous about my observation of her teaching. She explained that she had a perfect observation for several years and wanted to keep that intact. I explained that perfect observations were difficult, and our conversation went south. After she left my office, the rumor soon spread that everyone would be marked as needing improvement, put on growth plans, or fired. You can imagine what other people were saying about me.

Another quicksand trap I fell into was thinking everyone was wired just like me regarding our professional growth. If someone is doing a better job than I am, I try to find out why they are successful. Aren't we responsible for our personal growth? If someone was doing something better than me, I should study or question how the person was accomplishing the same task I was struggling with. I asked my instructional leaders to do the same thing. I asked them to find out how comparable schools were outperforming us.

One instructional leader asked me, *"Don't people usually ask us what we are doing to be successful?"*

Everything I tried was failing.

Next, I wanted to build a true Professional Learning Community (PLC) on my campus. I am proud that the PLC is now the norm in most schools. I was pushing for this in 2014. However, I needed to communicate what a PLC was and the expectations of department planning. I felt that teachers naturally would understand that working together was the cornerstone of a strong PLC, so I failed to communicate my expectations for a strong PLC.

When I attended planning periods and teachers were absent or not collaborating, I inquired why. We took great pride in building a master schedule that allowed for standard planning time, but teachers weren't utilizing the time. I started holding staff members accountable for something needed for our student's success.

Again, looking back, I was not sure how clear I was with my expectations.

I found some of my staff members didn't want to share their work for various reasons. Some didn't know what they needed to share, and some realized they didn't have much to share.

As Brené Brown says, "Clear is kind, and unclear is unkind."

I was being unkind to my staff. They should have never had to read my mind to understand what I wanted. Most, if not all, teachers want to do what is expected. I was failing them by not communicating what I wanted.

I implemented a staff book study in year one. Only some were ready for this. I ended up having to scale back. Looking back, I would have waited until year two for this.

As the year progressed, the culture continued to slip. I could feel it, and I couldn't catch a break. I received some advice from a staff member about teachers showing up late to work. While the expectation was for teachers to be on time, I didn't treat them with the respect that comes with being a professional. Now, instead of focusing on academic areas, I was watching for which teachers arrived five minutes late. Usually, I would not have done this, but I was grasping at straws to regain some improvements in campus culture.

But everything I did was working against me. I had to address teachers for failing to enter grades or return emails in a timely fashion. This is part of their job, but I had to address it, and some good people had their feelings hurt.

The culture was deteriorating by the day.

How did I get here? Looking back, my lack of communication was my quicksand. During my first principalship, I was failing miserably. Everything I tried seemed to backfire. I thought about quitting many times. I started to gain weight, and I began to neglect my family. I wasn't having fun at my job. I don't know what I would have done if it wasn't for the outstanding student body.

This is part of the administrative overwhelm that destroys leaders today. While I felt prepared for the job, I wasn't. Honestly, nothing prepares you for the job except the job. But I didn't give up. I had never been a quitter and wouldn't start then. I was determined to win back the staff.

First, I had to look in the mirror and reflect on what I could control. After all of that, I survived the first year. Some teachers left, I hired well, and I self-reflected on what I wanted for my campus culture. I thought about how I would communicate with staff over the summer. I thought long and hard about the crafting of my message. I made it a point to build upon people and not programs. I decided to slow down and listen to my staff.

In year two, I aimed to show who I was as a leader. I looked for ways to say yes to staff members. I trusted my staff and sought input from the irreplaceable staff members before implementing anything. I began designing the Triangle of Success and took every opportunity to explain my why and purpose. Things got better because I got better. In year two at Bradley Middle School, I focused on the campus's culture and climate.

When I was promoted to the principal of Churchill High School, the campus culture was thriving. Job satisfaction was high, and teachers enjoyed coming to work each day. I had learned from my first year what not to do as I entered the halls of the high school. But what else did I learn about leadership during year number one?

At the end of that school year, I got a tattoo of a star, the cross, and the word family on my forearm. The tattoo reminded me to keep everything in perspective. The star was my guiding light and what I was striving for. The tattoo was a constant reminder to put what matters at the forefront of my decision-making and to let everything else fall where it may. A colleague shared this advice with me, "Do not listen to criticism from someone you wouldn't take advice from."

Teddy Roosevelt once delivered a famous speech called "The Man in the Arena." If you are not familiar with the speech, it is excellent and speaks to our job as school leaders when it comes to dealing with criticism. President Roosevelt said,

> It is not the critic who counts: not the man who points out how the strong man stumbles or where the doer of deeds could have done better. The credit belongs to the man who is actually in the arena, whose face is marred by dust and sweat and blood, who strives valiantly, who errs and comes up short again and again, because there is no effort without error or shortcoming, but who knows the great enthusiasms, the great devotions, who spends himself in a worthy cause; who, at best, knows, in the end, the triumph of high achievement, and who, at the worst, if he fails, at least he fails while daring greatly so that his place shall never be with those cold and timid souls who knew neither victory nor defeat.

While many of the problems I have written about were my fault, I had to focus on the positive changes I had made during my first year. However, educators are often very self-reflective and hard on themselves. Educators focus on that one negative email and ignore the five positive ones. This is how we are wired. We are our own worst enemies.

If you notice, I didn't share anything positive. During my first year, we established Professional Learning Communities. We stressed relevant professional development that addressed the changing demographics of our community. We utilized social media to tell our story and craft our narrative. We hired administrators, counselors, and teachers that matched our vision. Our parent support and involvement continued to climb. Our students were happy and active and continued to excel academically. We committed ourselves to what was necessary. We found and charted a path toward our North Star: student achievement and success. I often wonder what it would be like to do it over again. Luckily, I was given that opportunity.

What is different now, a decade later? Well, for one, *I am different*. I have learned to listen more and slow down, literally and figuratively. I have learned to ask questions and trust the voice of irreplaceable teachers. I have learned to trust and delegate tasks to my staff. I have learned not to let the opinion of a disgruntled employee affect my sleep or my happiness while at home. I am also better at communicating my vision for how I want the culture of our campus to look and feel.

As staff, we developed core values. These core values were not just a sign that hung on a wall. They were something we lived. We revisited them and honored those staff members who were shining examples of them. We hired with our core values in mind. I highlighted staff and students who lived our core values. Faculty meetings started with these celebrations.

The core values became vital in helping us communicate what we expected of each other. While I was at Bradley, we also developed a definition of defeating behaviors based on the core values and discussed how these behaviors worked against our mission.

I learned that every opportunity I had to speak to my faculty, I needed to reiterate our why! I took the responsibility of creating the narrative of our campus personally. I didn't want any more surprises or quicksand on my campus. Nobody was going to have to read my mind.

As I transitioned to my new role as principal of a high school with 2,400 students, I reflected on my blueprint for guidance and reread my writings. I wanted to avoid repeating my mistakes from my first year. I learned that hiring and retaining the right people was critical to the school's success. This was also extremely important when developing my leadership team.

I hired Mr. Hector Perales in the 2019-2020 school year. Every leadership team needs a team member like Mr. Perales. He is fiercely loyal, hard-working, and never watches the clock. He built strong relationships with staff, students, and the community. An assistant principal who can connect with all stakeholders is crucial to success. His success allowed me to be successful. While he has the tools to be a principal, he has no desire to sit in the big chair, and that is just fine with me.

This chapter helped develop my entry plan and my chances of success during my second principalship. I needed to share my journey because it was therapeutic for me. While the word vulnerable became a cliché, I needed to humble myself to experience the success I knew I could have. To move forward, you must address the past. Please heed my warnings.

So, what did we do on campus to bring the culture back to where it is now?

Here's my list:

1. One interaction at a time
2. Why. Do. Have.
3. Onboarding
4. The Recharge Zone
5. Thank you cards
6. Treat every adult like family and believe that their intentions are well-intended.
7. Hire with culture in mind.

1. ONE INTERACTION AT A TIME

Doorway conversations are critical whether you are a new administrator or a veteran. These quiet moments help build trust, model positive interactions, and begin to shape the campus culture you want.

At Bradley, if I was going to win back the trust and re-establish the family culture on my campus, I had to let them know who I was. I accomplished this by getting to know the staff one teacher at a time and one doorway conversation at a time.

As I moved to high school, I made it my mission to visit every building and classroom daily. With almost 200 teachers, this was a constant challenge. Visibility is vital in building culture. How many of your staff members can say that they see you every day? Sadly, when teachers don't see us, you know what they say about us, don't you?

In my second year at Bradley, I said hello to teachers by name each time I saw them. I stopped and talked when teachers gave me the opportunity. I asked about family and tried to get to know them. I complimented them on classroom activities that I saw and asked for their input on topics I debated. I continued this each day and visited every section of the building to at least say hello to everyone. I would ask questions like:
"How is your son doing?"
"I saw your daughter's team won last night!"

"How about them Spurs?" or "How is your fantasy team doing?"

These small interactions allowed me to start opening doors. I laughed with the staff, laughed at my mistakes, and apologized to staff members if I felt I had wronged them. I spent my second year making amends through private conversations. One interaction at a time.

Some teachers didn't allow me to engage in discussions. I didn't push it, which motivated me to try again the following day. Over that year, I built solid relationships with the staff. I could feel the turn in the tide. I was hoisting myself out of the quicksand.

During my first semester as a high school principal, I implemented the same philosophy with hallway conversations. They allowed me to get to know the staff and student body. I routinely heard from the students that they enjoyed seeing me in the hallway or thanked me for being friendly and approachable. I spoke to every student that I passed in the hallway. I gave high fives, fist bumps, and smiles to every kid. I modeled this behavior for staff because I was shocked at the number of adults who passed kids and didn't interact with them – not in my school!

During conversations with staff, I asked about students and offered teachers support. If a teacher needed help with a student, I handled it right then. If I knew a student could have a discipline problem, I visited those classes and ensured students knew why I was there. Being visible on campus allowed me to establish trust with the staff.

Since one of my campus beliefs at Churchill was continued growth, I started sharing articles, books, and blogs during these interactions. I discussed using social media as a tool to grow as educators. I offered to connect educators with other educators I knew could assist them. As I became more and more trusted, they valued my opinion on instructional concerns.

> *"You need to be you from the beginning, day one. If you are not, you will never be able to keep up with the charade, which will be exhausting. So say it, show it, and do it without hesitation from your interview to each day you leave your car in the parking lot. And say it to them as a group, repeat it like a broken record, and write it on anything you can, any chance you can. Don't be ashamed. Don't be afraid. Don't hesitate. Never look back because you doubt your core, but look back often to ensure anyone walks with you!"*
>
> Crystal Romero-Mueller
Administrator, Houston, TX

In my first email to the Winston Churchill High School staff, I shared that my goal was to greet every teacher by first name daily. By publicly declaring my plan, the staff knew that I needed to be visible and get to see the team. When I moved to the high school in the spring Semester of 2019, I implemented the "one interaction at a time" approach to building trust on the campus. I pushed myself to visit every building on campus and made it a point to interact with every teacher and student.

Make time to visit every teacher's classroom every day! The visibility and the discussions will help craft the culture you desire.

2. WHY – DO – HAVE

We always tell our teachers that their students should never have to read their minds about what they want. Hence, the Clear is Kind motto while leading Churchill High School. The same is true with my staff. If I had taken the time upfront to communicate (and over-communicate) my core values and beliefs, I would have had a much smoother experience. You might be familiar with the coaching model of happiness Be, Do, Have. Essentially, the model challenges you to **Be** happy, and when you are happy, you will **Do** what you need to do to **Have** the things you want. While I love this model, I have made an adjustment that helped me shape and communicate my vision for the campus.

Our jobs can be stressful, and we often deal with negative and sad situations. If we allow this, we can become jaded. Each day I walk onto campus, I make it my mission to find joy in my job. I look for ways to seek happiness, frequently involving interacting with students and staff. I choose to be happy and do things to allow myself the happiness I seek. When I follow this model, I have what I need to be successful in my job.

I have also developed a variation of the Be, Do, Have model.

Communicate you**r why.**
Do what you say you are going to do.
You will then **have** everything you need to be successful and happy!

If you ask my staff right now, they will tell you that I am a champion of our school, students, and staff. They will tell you I love the historical pride of our campus and that I have found my dream job. They will tell you that our educators must reflect on practices, collaborate with colleagues, and improve their craft. Last, they will tell you I put family first in everything I do. (They may add that I have too much energy and should stop drinking caffeine.)

In all my correspondence with my staff, I ensure these themes are embedded in each message. When I first spoke to the staff at Churchill High School, I shared that my job was to cut the red tape to let them teach. I said I wasn't a micromanager (unless needed) and trusted them to be outstanding teachers.

Some leaders believe our job is to hire great people and get out of their way! I told the staff that my job was to hire and retain great people AND walk with them on their journey. Why would I want to get out of their way? I want to walk alongside these outstanding educators as they do what we hired them to do! Nothing energizes me more than seeing an exceptional educator in action.

I then needed to ensure that I was practicing what I was preaching. The staff was watching. Did I walk the walk? Or was I just repeating some educational buzzwords and was full of myself? I had to ensure that I was modeling what I expected my staff to live up to. I championed my community, team, and students through social media. I truly felt that if I didn't tell the stories of Bradley Middle School and Churchill High School, someone else would. "If you do not provide the narrative, one will be provided for you." This was some of the best advice I have ever received. It came from Dr. Alex Flores from Trinity University in San Antonio. Think about that statement for a moment. If I don't shout out all the positives of my campus from the mountaintop, who will? I had a parent stop me and jokingly ask, "Do you believe everything you say about our campus being so special?" The answer was *absolutely!*

My staff knows that I am also active in continuous learning. I take my professional development very seriously. I love to attend conferences and connect. I am an active blogger, and my staff knows I have been working on *The Blueprint* for years. As I modeled this growth, many teachers shared books they read or activities they were proud of.

While I stressed prioritizing family, I also had to ensure I was modeling this. This was difficult, and I still need help with this area. Neglecting your family can quickly become a habit. I include my family in many events to ensure I do not neglect my wife and kids. I share stories about my family, kids, and weekend plans in all my emails. I start every weekly staff email with what the Bloomer family did over the weekend. While I enjoy bragging about my family, it also gives my staff a glimpse into who I am.

Another simple tip came from a colleague of mine. I recently went for a walk in a park close to my neighborhood. As I was beginning, I encountered Coach Glen Hill and his wife, Holly, out walking. While I walked with them, Coach Hill said something very profound. "Holly and I like to take walks. During the walk, we can solve a lot of problems." Spend time with your family and loved ones!

Every school proclaims that they are a family. But do our actions match our words? Throughout the year, a teacher may approach you and ask, "Can I come in after first period tomorrow? I want to see my son in his play at school."

"Yes."

Dr. Bobby Martinez believes in putting your family first. To demonstrate this, he has covered classes for teachers who needed to attend an event for their children. Do you think anyone at his school will ever question whether he values family?

Former middle school principal Dr. Herb Cox made it a point for his teachers with young children to be able to take their kids to school on the first day of school. He believed this was important and would often cover a class to make this happen.

When your staff knows you love family and will support them however you can, you build the thriving school culture you desire. When you live by the Why, Do, Have Philosophy, you will be on the right track to creating the campus culture you want.

3. ONBOARDING

It is crucial to lay out the expectations of any organization upfront. One of my favorite TV shows is Seinfeld. In a classic episode, George is terminated for having a romantic encounter on his desk at work. When he meets with his boss and is fired, he replies, "Was that wrong?" While we all know that George knew this was wrong, it illustrates the need for clarity in the onboarding process.

I have referenced my trips to Silicon Valley throughout *The Blueprint*. The mission of these trips was to study the culture and climate of the companies and replicate what they do in our schools. At each company, I inquired how they could be certain that the culture they wanted continued. Each company stressed the importance of its onboarding process as the key to its success. This process ensured that new employees fully understood the company's expectations.

Clear is kind.

Their focus on the onboarding process made me review and discuss the support we offered new staff members. Especially during a teacher shortage, we had to ensure that we kept all our new teachers.

Most campuses pair a new teacher with a mentor teacher and provide monthly meetings that review and discuss ongoing events. This information is all that is needed for some teachers new to campus. For others, more guidance is necessary. More and more of our candidates are applying for jobs as alternative certification candidates, which means they missed student teaching and experiencing a semester of what it is like to be a teacher. Is a monthly meeting and a teacher mentor enough?

It is unfair to expect a new teacher to be held to the same standard as a veteran teacher if we do not invest the time and energy into their development. In Chapter One, I spoke of new teachers as irreplaceables. They are eager and often idealistic. As we address the nationwide teacher shortage crisis, we must support every teacher, especially the new teachers. We have to retain every new teacher. We can't let them leave.

At Churchill High School, we met every Friday with new teachers during the first marking period. Not only did we present to the cohort on essential topics, but we also intentionally built family within this group. As the principal, I attended every meeting. I spoke about our core values and tried to add humor. I had them share what was working well for them, and I noticed if someone wasn't doing well during these weekly check-ins. I also met individually with each new teacher for about 30 minutes during the first marking period. While I had a few questions, each session had a different flow. In these meetings, I ensured that each teacher knew how much I believed in them and their success as teachers.

As I mentioned, I shared an email with my new teachers every Friday at 8:30 AM. This was separate and different from my weekly staff emails. I took a fatherly approach in these emails to support and grow teachers. I also utilized a strategy I learned from Todd Whitaker.
In keeping with the theme of crafting and driving the narrative, I took liberties to talk about "great teachers." I shared best practices and campus initiatives I wanted to see in the classroom to benefit students. I would often say, "Our best teachers are implementing…"
I hoped the new teachers would want to emulate the great teachers.

As the building principal and instructional leader, I visit every new teacher at least once a week. During these visits, I always leave written feedback on an index card or a sticky note. We must work alongside and support our new teachers in the classroom. I will never let a new teacher fail!

I implore you to review and analyze the processes that you have in place to support new teachers. At Churchill, we refer to an approach to going the extra mile for students or colleagues as *Doing it the Churchill Way*. But if we are not implicitly modeling and supporting what the Churchill way looks like for new teachers, how are they learning what we expect?

4. THE RECHARGE ZONE

During the summers of 2017 and 2019, while traveling to Silicon Valley, I discovered one way that leading companies were taking care of their employees that I could duplicate in my school.

Principal John Hinds set up visits and debriefs with some top executives from Apple, Google, Stanford's School of Education, IDEO, Airbnb, Cisco, Aruba, HP, and One WorkPlace. These remarkable, behind-the-scenes visits and discussions allowed a group of principals from San Antonio, Texas, to pick their brains and bring back notebooks filled with ideas. Many of these leading companies were providing perks to their employees. From providing food to changing the oil in their car while at work, these bonuses make the work experience unique.

Inspired by the California companies, I now wanted to focus on the perks I could provide my staff. I thought, "I can't pay my teachers any more than I already do, but what can I do to reward them and give them perks that no other campuses have?" During a briefing with members from Airbnb, they stressed how the company took care of people. This simple statement resonated with me for weeks. Employees know when their companies take care of them.

In each discussion with an executive from Google or IDEO, I studied what they wore, what was on the wall, and what was offered to employees regarding food and beverages. Based on everything I learned, I implemented the ReCharge Zone. My goal was to have coffee and fruit-infused water daily for my staff. I envisioned putting out breakfast bars and bags of chips throughout the day. My secretary originally wanted to put the ReCharge Zone in the lounge. However, I preferred the ReCharge Zone outside my office to continue building staff relationships over food and through conversation. When staff members visited the ReCharge Zone, I could also visit with them and continue building upon our campus culture. I wanted this to be a place for teachers to swing by during their conference period.

Because great conversations occur around food and drink, I made it a point to visit with staff members who came by for a fill-up. Through these quiet conversations, I made meaningful connections with staff members.

I needed to figure out how to fund this idea. Private companies like Google could pay for these perks, but school districts can't pay for food and drink. I knew this was a great idea to build upon improvements in campus culture and one that would be greatly appreciated. I contacted our neighborhood grocery store, HEB. After explaining my plan for the ReCharge Zone, I found an excellent partner in Sonia Flores, the store's Unit Director. She sponsored me each month with gift cards to help fund the project.

I also found willing business partners throughout my community. All I had to do was ask them to drop off food and coupons or offer their services to our staff. I asked teacher organizations and other professional groups that wanted to use our campus if they wanted to contribute to the ReCharge Zone.

On the first day of school, I set up the ReCharge Zone outside my office on a table. I brewed a massive pot of coffee and made lemon-infused water. I had donuts and other breakfast food on the table. As teachers came by during their conference period, they could fill up coffee or their water bottles. I made it a point to talk with everyone who utilized the ReCharge Zone. While the staff was filling up their coffee mugs, I was working on building trust and crafting the culture I wanted on my campus.

Organically, the ReCharge Zone evolved. Teachers began to notice the hard work required to maintain and stock the zone. They started dropping off baked goods and cans of coffee. One teacher donated limes from his backyard. The ReCharge zone became a source of pride for the campus and a positive part of our culture. It evolved from year one to year two. A few times a semester, I made chips and queso. As I wandered the campus, I let teachers know what they could find at the zone. Nothing made me happier than seeing teachers taking bowls of queso with chips back to their class for a snack throughout the day. Their smiles showed me that the culture was turning.

Without an announcement, I would make pancakes and have them out for teachers as they came into work. A few times, we made sausages to go along with the breakfasts. This simple treat was well received. The extra time it took me to cook that morning was well worth it. I bought a toaster oven from a garage sale and made cheese hot dogs. I also bought pizza rolls or frozen pizzas and cooked them.

I couldn't afford to do this for the entire staff, but what I wanted to create was a desire to visit the office (to see what the ReCharge Zone had). I would make 12 hot dogs and cut them in half. For the first 24 that visited the office, I had snack-sized hot dogs. I cut frozen pizzas into small squares. On these days, I was only looking to provide a snack for the teachers and not a meal.

The ReCharge Zone became vital to a powerful culture change on my campus. While the approach required some effort on my part, it made positive changes in attitude and behavior.

5. THANK YOUR FACULTY AND STAFF FOR WHAT THEY DO

To continue building upon the desired campus culture, I knew I needed to communicate to my staff how much I appreciated them. If we don't show appreciation and let staff know that we see them, value them, and couldn't do it without them, they will leave our school or our profession. Teachers are in control. It is a teacher's market, and they can negotiate what grade level or subject they teach. In the summer of 2023, I hired a math teacher who indicated he only wanted to teach a specific math section. He knew I would make it happen if I wanted him at Churchill. We made it happen, and he joined the Churchill family. So, how do you keep teachers from leaving your campus at the end of the year?

You can never underestimate the power of thanking and acknowledging adults for a well-done job. As I moved around the campus and visited every teacher daily, I made it a point to thank staff members for being at their door during passing periods or attending a game or concert the evening before. I also ensured that I visited the directors and coaches and thanked them for their hard work.

Brian Buffini, the self-made millionaire, author, and speaker, writes ten thank-you notes every morning. His administrative assistant places the cards on his keyboard each morning. If Mr. Buffini doesn't get the ten cards written on Monday, he has twenty to write on Tuesday. He realizes the importance of a handwritten card.

We start every leadership meeting by writing a thank you card to a staff member. Seeing those cards hanging on the wall near the teacher's desk when I walk through a classroom is heartwarming. We all know that employees who feel valued and supported will work harder. We also know that when employees feel underappreciated, they quietly quit while still on the job. One of my former assistant principals, Ms. Jennifer Jones, designed specially made Valentine's cards for each teacher. These were a massive hit with the staff.

Dr. Lance Groppel realizes the importance of writing thank-you notes. The first five minutes of Dr. Groppel's weekly leadership staff meetings are devoted to writing thank-you notes to staff members. Dr. Groppel tracks the messages to ensure every staff member receives a genuine handwritten card. I have since incorporated this practice into all of my leadership team meetings. The most effective thank you notes were precise, sincere, and included something unique to the person.

I sent a personalized text message to every staff member each summer before the start of each year. While it might not have the warmth of handwritten cards, these interactions continued to forge strong relationships with the staff. While some of them were easier than others, this forced me to find a connection with each staff member.

In February 2024, our school had a student win a gold medal at the state swim meet. I took a picture of her and texted it to her teachers, thanking them for supporting and teaching a state champion. I feel like these interactions and these thank-yous helped shape the culture I was striving for.

6. TREAT EVERY ADULT LIKE A FAMILY MEMBER AND BELIEVE THEIR INTENTIONS ARE GENUINE

From the custodian who opens the campus in the morning to the teacher who recently filed a grievance against you, every adult deserves to be treated as if they were family.

Think about your family for a moment. If a family member needed something, you would do anything to help, am I right? This mindset is necessary when working to help your staff members succeed. If a staff member has a family event, I look for coverage that allows them to leave early to assist a family member. I always look for ways to say yes to any family issue.

During my first year, I mentioned that I received bad advice from a staff member about cracking down on teachers showing up late. After dealing with the fallout, I decided to take a different approach. I now assume that if a teacher shows up a few minutes late for work, there is a good intention and reason why they are late. You can't show up late every day, but life happens. My family and I are late to almost every family gathering we must attend. Family = School.

A teacher who was an active critic of mine showed up to work about thirty minutes late one day. This wasn't normal. Every bone in my body wanted to call this teacher in and document it. Before I could even find the teacher, I received an email explaining the reason behind the delay. I am glad I chose the high road and did not call her into my office and wag my finger at her.

7. HIRE WITH YOUR CULTURE IN MIND

This practice became crucial for changing the culture on every campus I have ever worked. If you hire great people with your campus vision and culture in mind, you will turn the corner. The only way an organization improves is through its people. Hiring is something we control as educators. Our job is to hire intelligently and with culture in mind.

In the summer of 2017, I hired an alternative certified teacher named Sherman Roberts to teach and coach. I had known Sherman for ten years as he coached my son in Catholic Youth Organization (CYO) basketball. I admired how Sherman worked with the kids and knew he was a natural teacher and coach. Sherman was in the business sector then, and every time I saw him, I would actively recruit him to teach and coach.

He was a pied piper when it came to kids. They naturally flocked to him. He was a magnet. He was the kind of guy I wanted on campus because of his kind heart and desire to connect with kids. I knew he would learn his role as a SpEd teacher. Do you think there was any doubt that Coach Roberts wasn't successful? Find educators like Coach Roberts to help shape your campus culture. I hired him because we need caring people who love kids. As I started to improve my staff, I realized the importance of the hiring process. I needed to continue adding great people to my team.

At Churchill High School, I relied on my irreplaceable teachers to also help recruit teachers to join our family. My deans of each core content department would bring to me individuals they knew would fit our culture. I hired an elementary school teacher for a special education position in the summer of 2023. She was an excellent teacher. She came to me around Thanksgiving and said she was actively recruiting like-minded individuals to join our family because she loved being at Churchill.

Your current teachers are a precious resource for recruiting teachers who fit your campus culture and climate. If a teacher liked being at Churchill, enjoyed the respect and autonomy they were given to do their job, and felt it was a positive culture, wouldn't they only want to recruit those just like them? To hire while keeping culture at the forefront, I write questions with our campus culture in mind. I design the questions to find empathic people who believe in lifelong learning and desire a family-like atmosphere.

We can teach teachers the nuts and bolts of the job, but we cannot teach teachers how to care or be empathetic. What I can't teach is caring for kids. A campus can provide curriculum, classroom management strategies, and data-debriefs to any teacher. Through mentorship, we can deliver relevant examples of how to work with gifted and talented students, emerging bilingual students, or students with special education services. But what I can't teach is how to care for a student who lost their father. I can't teach empathy for a student working part-time to support their family and struggling academically. I can't teach someone how to give a second chance. I can't teach being a good teammate to your peers.

So, how do you hire candidates that fit your requirements? The key here is designing questions that allow you to find candidates that fit your culture. Do you have a question that cuts to the core of what you want to create on your campus? When you craft your questions around what matters, the candidates who fit your campus will rise to the top. I have devoted all of Chapter Six to the hiring process.

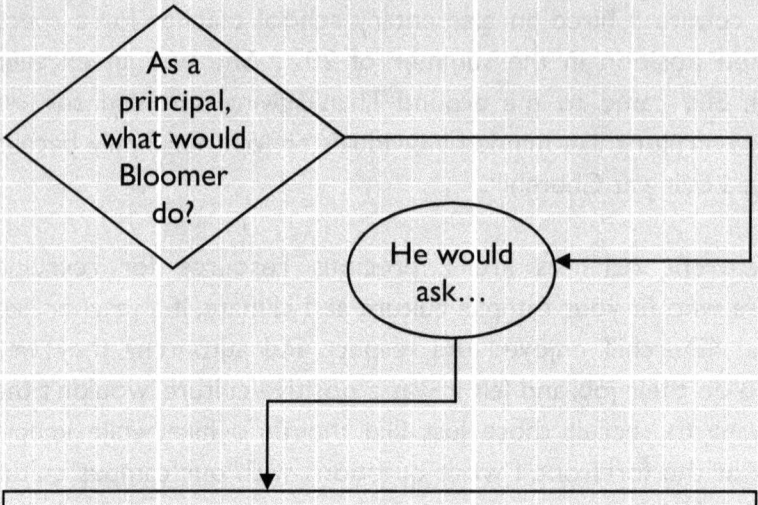

- If I asked a random teacher from your campus about your core values and beliefs, would the person know them?
- Recall your last few interactions with teachers. Did you take advantage of these opportunities to share your values, share your joy for the job, and leave teachers inspired to do the work?

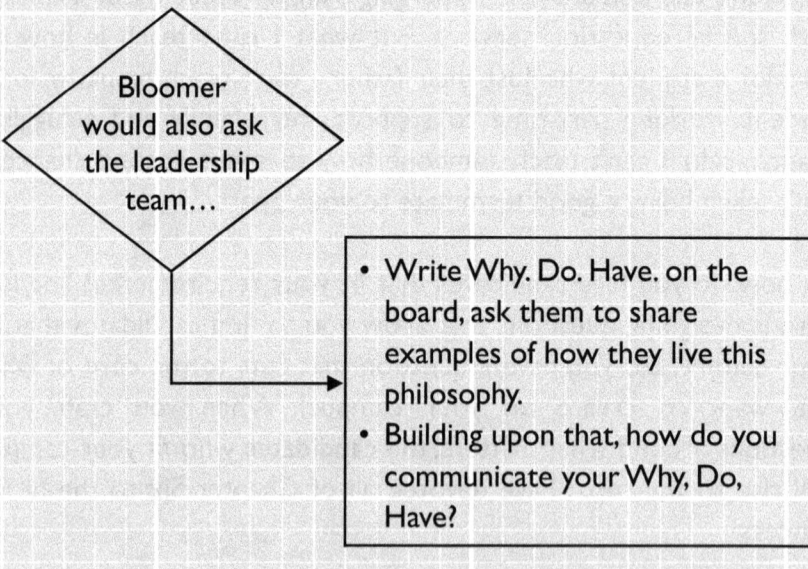

- Write Why. Do. Have. on the board, ask them to share examples of how they live this philosophy.
- Building upon that, how do you communicate your Why, Do, Have?

119

CHAPTER 4
Disrupting the Status Quo & Leading for Change

Social media has been a game changer for me as an educator. It has exposed me to ideas and philosophies I might never have been privy to. Engaging with the top educators in the nation has given me the confidence to push the envelope and challenge the status quo. It has also allowed me to see a new status quo, which our community deserves.

Have you ever stopped to think about the term status quo? We talk much about it in education, but how do we define it? And while we are on the topic, does the status quo always need to be disrupted? If a practice has been occurring on campus for the past twenty years, does that make it outdated, or does that make it part of the campus fabric?

If you look up the definition of status quo in Webster's dictionary, you will find that it means the current situation or how things are now. That doesn't sound good or bad, does it? Through the lens of the blueprint, the status quo can be looked at in various ways. It doesn't always have to be harmful; it can be good, depending on how you interrupt the status quo. If your school's culture continuously improves, the status quo should continue. This is healthy and should never be discontinued.

Under the guidance of head coach Gregg Popovich, the San Antonio Spurs of the NBA are a perfect example of an organization that maintains the status quo. They have done so for the last twenty years. To the Spurs, the status quo is acquiring players that fit their system. When players join the Spurs family, they realize that they are part of something bigger than themselves. Coach Popovich and his management team have a clear vision and know where they want to go. In a day and age when athletes are focused on their stats, the Spurs focus on a team-first approach. The Spurs were the first to capitalize on bringing European players to the NBA. Names like Tony Parker and Manu Ginobili are common now because of how the Spurs did business. Their strategy was one of constant improvement and constant evaluation. This is the exception to the rule.

If the culture of your campus is to blame students or an area of the city that the school resides in, then the status quo needs to be disrupted immediately! I have always believed that the zip code a student resides in should not be a learning disability.

Status quo can also relate to the instructional practices on the campus that do not meet the student body's needs. If this is the case, the status quo must be destroyed.

So, why do schools still look almost exactly as they did when I was a student? Sadly, the status quo can be very comfortable. We all enjoy being cozy. When in doubt, we often resort to comfort in times of stress and uncertainty. I also firmly believe we don't know what we don't know.

Teachers who live in their comfort zones may not know any better. You can't hold them accountable for something they don't know. If you want to change, you must show them something different and more effective.

With more and more teachers entering the profession as alternative teaching candidates, we must ensure we work closely with them. Without the student teaching experience, a new teacher might resort to how they learned as a student. This might be by straight lecture throughout the week, then a test on Friday. This isn't their fault; they just don't know better until we show them a better way!

As I mentioned previously, it is our moral imperative to provide our students with the education that each of them deserves. We have been appointed as principals to push the envelope and disrupt where and what needs to be disrupted. We are disruptors! We are game-changers!

> "The status quo bar we are setting is that ALL students can and will be successful. That EVERY STUDENT will achieve at high levels. Our mission statement ends with 'EVERY STUDENT – EVERY MINUTE – EVERY DAY.' We believe that we must have a meaningful impact on the lives of ALL our students. This is done not only to close the opportunity gaps but also to close the expectation gaps for EVERY STUDENT.
>
> Shane Mckay
> Former High School Principal,
> East Central ISD, San Antonio, TX

We talk about being 21st-century educators all the time, but when this book was written, we were almost twenty-five years into the 21st century. What are we waiting for?

To lead change, we have to show the way. We must model the way for our leadership team, staff, and community. We must let them know that we will never settle for average and that our school can be the focal point of real change. We have to believe it! Next time someone asks you what you do, tell them you are an Educational Disruptor!

If we want to implement systemic change in our schools, we must show the way and paint a picture of what it could look like. We must let our stakeholders know what we want, what we need, and what we expect! We have to paint a picture so vivid that everyone can see it.

If I, as the building principal, am not championing my school as something special, how can I expect my staff to do the same? We are at the most exciting time in the history of education. We are the captains of the ships that will forever change the way students are educated. Our families are counting on us to prepare their children for jobs that must be created.

COVID has allowed us as educators to finally address the inadequacies we have permitted in education for decades. Jennifer Gutierrez, an administrator in San Antonio, describes her new status quo.

> "To me, the new status quo is a community of learners working to meet the specific needs of the students that attend that school daily. Do whatever it takes to ensure your staff, students, and parents have what they need to meet the needs of the students successfully. Our schools were created for students; the environment and decisions should revolve around what is best for them."

> "The new status quo, in my opinion, is that educators must care for and care about one another and every person we come into contact with daily. We face many challenges, funding concerns, charters, choice, etc. The time long ago when everyone just sent their children to the neighborhood school is a thing of the past. The new status quo is we have to make our schools the place to be."

Mrs. Julie Shore
Executive Director of Fine Arts, North East ISD

So, how do you determine what is next for your campus? You must check your campus's temperature to determine the status quo.

I encourage you to listen to your irreplaceables to determine the ground truths of your campus. They will paint a picture for you of exactly what you have. This is also a prime opportunity to implement the Triangle of Success to determine your campus's health. We must seek out the voices of our stakeholders.

What I discovered as a high school principal was loud and clear. My staff wanted the pride and traditions highlighted on the campus. I could do that! Our school has over fifty years of tradition. Our traditions and people made us different from any other campus I had ever stepped foot on. Without the customs, we were just an average school. Every chance I had, I talked about pride and traditions. We brought back former Churchill Chargers and had them speak about what it meant to them to work on our campus.

> "... the 'new status quo' depends on the campus because it differs for every campus. I think it is the role of the principal to collaborate and develop what that new status quo is and how we reshape culture."
>
> Dr. Lance Groppel
> Deputy Superintendent of Administration
> Tyler ISD, Tyler, TX

Have you seen the movie *Back to the Future* with Michael J. Fox? Fox's character accidentally travels back in time and must ensure that his parents meet so that he is born thirty years later. The 80s comedy could also be an excellent analogy to walking into a school in the 1950s and today. You would expect the two schools, decades apart, to look different. But they are not much different.

It wouldn't shock us to walk into a 1950s class and see the teacher lecturing to students sitting in rows and taking notes. Now, fast forward to 2024. What would you see in most classrooms? Would it shock you to see many classrooms still in rows, with the teacher lecturing from the front of the class and assigning worksheets or packets? The only difference might be cell phones in the students' hands.

I asked my wife, who is not an educator, the following question: Pretend you are a teacher for one day. You are going to teach US history about the Revolutionary War. You can do anything you want. How would you teach? "I would have notes on a PowerPoint and give them a quiz at the end to see if they grasped all the information. I might show a movie," she said. My wife has never had any training to be a teacher. Did she just describe most of a student's day in school? Notes, assess, move on. Notes, assess, move on. Occasionally, show a movie. Will this approach meet the changing students that are arriving on campus?

Stop for a moment. I graduated high school in 1992. When I was in middle school and high school, I would have bet money that our schools in 2024 would have been closer to the futuristic Jetsons than what my New York State school looked like. How do we have Apple Music, Netflix, Uber, DoorDash, and many other technological advances that we would have never considered in 1992, but our classrooms haven't changed?

When I was a student, most children came to school from homes that valued public education. Most of my friends had two parents, and they were held accountable for being successful in school. Their parents also stressed going to college. Growing up:
    I never knew a friend who was abused.
    I never had a friend die by suicide.
    I didn't have friends who couch surfed at night because they didn't have a place to stay.

I didn't have friends stealing and selling their parents' pills at school.
I didn't know any transgender kids.
I didn't know students who vaped THC each day.

Now, public schools have become a microcosm of our society. We are welcoming and accepting. Public schools have always welcomed, accepted, and educated every student. We now have children in our schools and walking our hallways carrying severe baggage – much more than we might ever know.

My high school in San Antonio, Texas, had about 50 students from Latin America enroll during the spring of 2022. With global political turmoil, our schools are seeing more refugees enroll.

Schools now have students from around the globe, often sitting in the same class. While diversity adds uniqueness, it also presents numerous challenges. I now use Google Translate each day. I recently used Russian to communicate with a new student.

Since the tragedy in Uvalde, Texas, in May of 2022, our new status quo revolves around locked doors. While school safety has always been a concern, I would argue that it is now more important than chemistry or world geography. We now practice school shooter drills like they are fire drills. We teach kids as young as elementary school to look for items to throw at a potential school shooter. Every one of these issues is extremely important to me as an educator. But how can we adequately address every issue brought to our doorstep?

The role of the principal is becoming unmanageable. This is why the educational system is at a tipping point, and we need strong leadership now more than ever. Our new status quo involves providing appropriate education to *all* children. Every student I just described deserves a grade-level education. The new status quo revolves around dealing with students who are endlessly connected.

Snapchat, Instagram, and Twitter allow people to stay in touch with the touch of a screen. Students have all the music they need in their pockets, and their headphones are a vital lifeline.

> ❝ *The new status quo revolves around students used to on-demand access to everything in their lives.* ❞

How does a teacher take these mitigating factors and provide a lesson for their students? Dr. James Barton, Superintendent of Caldwell ISD in Texas, believes that "The new status quo for instruction is a refocus on engagement through technology, collaboration, and interaction."

Here is my educational vision for the new status quo:

> *Zoe walks toward her classroom. Her teacher greets her with a high five, a hug, and a smile. She enters the class and checks the board for the class assignment. Based on what is written on the board, Zoe determines that she wants to work in a comfy bean bag in the back. As she sits and unpacks her backpack, she takes out a snack and a bottle of water. She also takes out her Chromebook and logs into the Google Classroom the teacher has created. Her friends Tori and Andrew join her a few moments later. They do the same, and soon, the group will collaborate on a project they have been working on for the entire week. The teacher works with students in small groups during class, providing remediation and acceleration.*
>
> *This has been the students' favorite project of the year because the teacher gave them autonomy in showing mastery of the objectives. The group decided on the*

norms and conferenced with the teacher to ensure they were on the right track. The group agreed on checkpoints to ensure they would meet their deadline. The students continued their work at home and aced the assessment the teacher developed at the project's end. After the project, the kids felt like experts and begged the teacher to continue similar projects.

Doesn't this sound like a classroom you would have wanted to be in? Would you like your children in this classroom? Can you imagine what our schools would be like if this was the new status quo? Students graduating from this high school would be future-ready based on the ability to collaborate, work in groups, and accomplish a task at hand.

> *"We need to be accountable for our achievement and growing students, but that looks different for every kiddo in the building. What does your campus believe a successful student looks like, exiting the grade level and transitioning from elementary to middle school?"*
>
> *Stacy Kimbriel*
> *Elementary Principal, Plano, TX*

A parent asked me why I was spending time in California and what value touring Silicon Valley provided me as a building principal. The parent's question caused me to reflect and be clear about what I wanted for my campus. During our visits to the Valley, I didn't meet anyone that accepted mediocrity or excuses. These companies have a problem-solving mindset and a strong belief that any issue can be solved. Isn't this the philosophy we need as leaders to lead a campus successfully?

I often think about how Silicon Valley leaders would attack issues we have in schools. What would be their approach to closing the achievement gap or preparing students to be college, career, or military ready? The overwhelming belief system in Silicon Valley is that if they don't have the people to solve the problem, they find people who can solve it! They don't accept the status quo! They don't accept complacency, and they are true disruptors!

Things to consider when leading for change:

1. How do you handle the resistance?
2. Fly your flag!
3. Rally the troops.
4. Utilize data to support change.
5. Constantly explain why.
6. Create opportunities for your staff to grow.
7. Hire Purposefully and hire for change.
8. The time to change is when you are on top.

1. HOW TO HANDLE RESISTANCE TO CHANGING THE STATUS QUO

There will be resistance! Get ready for it!

If you are like me, you were ready to roll the minute you were named principal. Your mind started racing, and you were prepared to change the world! However, your moves must be calculated and transparent to ensure you can lead your campus into the new status quo. You must avoid repeating the same mistakes I made during my first tenure.

Remember, I mentioned in Chapter One that anything you do on campus will be new. If you are beginning to lay the groundwork for the new status quo, this will require great skill because you will face pushback from staff members.

"There will inherently be resistance. The key is to develop a critical mass that surrounds the initiative—having key campus leaders on board that ultimately drown out the naysayers. We don't pay attention to those who are 'just playing devil's advocate' faculty members. Those are the closet pessimists who parade around as 'realists.' We don't have time or energy to change their ways. Usually, we see it as insecurity they have about themselves, and it manifests as a naysayer."

Shane Mckay
Former High School Principal
East Central High School, San Antonio, TX

I failed to develop consensus during my first year as I began moving my school to prepare for the future. I should have communicated the urgency clearly but failed to rally my staff behind why we needed to disrupt the status quo.

"You will just go in knowing there will be resistors. You have to know who you are. You have to practice those conversations in advance (yes, go ahead and hold your phone while driving so that those who look at you think you're talking on the telephone…). You have to reflect on your conversations (yes, use the same strategy while driving home and replay the conversations in your mind and out loud) to know what you would say differently next time or need to follow up on to clarify communication that was exchanged."

Crystal Romero-Mueller
Administrator, Houston, TX

As you settle into your job, seeking guidance and input from your leadership team about the needs of your campus becomes critical.

Suppose you are a new principal, inheriting experienced administrators. In that case, you will need to lean on these administrators for their guidance and knowledge as you begin to lay out the new status quo.

I have seen administrative teams have honest discussions about teachers, departments, and grade-level teams. Are the right teachers teaching the "right" classes? Are your best teachers teaching the students with the most pressing needs? Are the right people in the right seats on the bus?

Dr. James Barton, Superintendent of Caldwell ISD in Texas, believes that during these meetings, the following needs to occur: "Identify organizational strengths to maintain and areas to address, find the strengths of others, and make sure they are in the right position." He suggests working on "shaping the culture of the building, from people to paint" during these meetings.

Schools often task their most effective teachers with teaching their academically strong students. While every student deserves a fantastic teacher, first-year teachers are often given to students in lower-level or remedial classes. The practice of assigning brand new teachers to the most vulnerable students needs to be eliminated.

During these discussions, ask each administrator what they would do if they were in your shoes. Listening to what each administrator values and deems essential should help you gather the big picture for the campus needs assessment. Be honest with your core leadership groups about what you seek from these discussions. Honesty is crucial in helping you establish trust and being transparent. Again, ask them what they would do if they were in your shoes. These suggestions and concerns could differ significantly from what your leadership team communicates. I also love to ask, "What advice do you have for me?" After gathering all your information, you should be able to develop a plan for dealing with the resistance.

Let's look at this scenario. You have brought the energy, met with your staff, and been insanely visible, but you still have resistance. Some staff members might take this approach: "I have had X number of principals, and they have all come and gone. I will just wait you out as well." Another popular response is, "I'll just close my door and do what I want."

The million-dollar question becomes this: How do you handle the resistance now? Stay consistent with your why, highlight the urgency, continue positive communication to the staff, students, and community and your door-to-door conversations with staff members.

I have known many administrators who have won over the naysayers by including them in decision-making. This approach often shows respect for staff members and lends credibility to the administrator. It might also rekindle a fire inside a disenchanted staff member.

Successful administrators who overcome resistance always maintain their focus on their mission. Resistance can be destroyed through conversations and day-to-day interactions. As I shared earlier, a lack of information allows doubt and misinformation to fill in the gaps. Great leaders craft their message and communicate it in a variety of ways.

Finally, those who can't or won't get on board will require a private conversation about their intentions. Sometimes, these staff members need to be counseled out of the school. We don't have time for someone to work against what is best for kids.

2. FLY YOUR FLAG

The most effective way to disrupt the status quo is to paint a picture of urgency around needed change. I refer to this concept as flying your flag. Your flag is your call to action to solve a severe problem. When everyone knows what they are fighting for, they can conceptualize the task and delineate the steps needed to accomplish the goal.

With the idea of calling attention to a problem, I point to the once-dominant Blockbuster Video Chain. Many of us can remember renting a video or DVD from the chain. Who would have thought that chain would be nonexistent in 2024? I often wonder if anyone within the organization voiced concerns about companies like Netflix, Hulu, or Amazon Prime Video. Did anyone raise a flag of worry? If they did, did anyone listen? We all know the answer to that question.

While this organization differs significantly from schools, their story should be considered as a case study for failure to adapt or change. With the rise of charter schools, public schools face competition they never have before. Parents and students have choices.

Fly your urgency flag as you begin to disrupt the status quo! Without the flag, your efforts for change will fail and fail miserably.

3. RALLY THE TROOPS

From experience, rallying the teachers to the urgency needed within a school is critical in successfully disrupting the status quo. You cannot do this alone. I tried during my first year, and I failed. You must rally key school community members to accomplish this transformation.

Leaders must realize that pushing educators out of their comfort zones requires a team approach. Your entire leadership team needs to be on the same page regarding the staff's urgency and rallying. If the campus leadership team does not feel urgency, you will fail to disrupt the status quo.

I have been blessed to work with administrators who have shared the same beliefs and sense of urgency that I have had with disrupting the status quo. However, I have also worked with administrators who find living in their comfort zone easier. They get caught up sitting at their desk and "playing office." Sadly, staff members know when they have an ineffective administrative team. What administrator worth their salt would stand by idly and allow a subpar education to be delivered to their students?

I am sure many administrators said in their interview that they would never allow this attitude in any school they served. But schools have been failing kids for decades.

By rallying the troops, a campus will succeed.

4. UTILIZE DATA TO SUPPORT CHANGE

Once you have met with your extended leadership teams and determined your course of action, data should become your best friend. Data can be your ace in the hole to disrupt the status quo. I have had to learn to love and appreciate data. It can help you break logjams on campus and create a sense of urgency.

As a teacher, if I had seen one more piece of data, I might have quit. There was only so much data I could comprehend, swallow, digest, and work with. But I realized that I was using data in all the wrong ways. Anyone can look at the data. What we do with the data is vital.

If your campus has instructional or state assessment shortfalls, the data will provide hotspots to address. For example, if you are teaching eighth grade social studies and your data reveals that students are struggling with cause and effect, that area should become an area of focus. This should encourage you to ask how cause and effect are taught since students are unsuccessful. This awareness should drive your instruction and planning.

xData should be reviewed and shared at PLC meetings. It should drive what is taught and how it is taught. Not only is it essential to analyze which standard students are struggling with but to allow the data to identify the students who would benefit from remediation on that standard. Data truly allows numbers and projections to come to life by putting a name and face to those numbers.

Professor John Hattie, an educational researcher from the University of Melbourne, has developed a list of over 250 factors that contribute to student growth. His top factor, which he believes can help a student grow by over a year and a half, is collective teacher efficacy. If this is the case, why wouldn't we look at our teachers preparing their students academically and study their practices, lessons, and strategies?

The book *Switch* by Chip and Dan Heath describes finding bright spots in organizations. By utilizing campus data, you can find bright spots within your school. You can capitalize on these bright spots to help motivate and inspire teachers to continue disrupting the status quo.

A principal is charged with being an instructional leader. Over the years, I have learned that a principal cannot do this monumental task alone. In studying schools that have closed achievement gaps and disrupted the status quo, I have found a robust professional learning community on these campuses. Teachers work together in these professional learning communities to address student learning. While many campuses have dedicated time to planning, a strong PLC analyzes student data to drive instruction and asks four questions while planning, all based on student data and student work:

1. What do we want the students to know and be able to do?
2. How will we know if they learned it?
3. What do we do if a student already knows the material?

4. What do we do for the students who do not know the material?

A school with a solid academic culture utilizes data to drive instruction.

When data reveals shortfalls, ask why. The data can also help you reveal which students were close to passing the state assessment and what interventions can be provided to those students throughout the year. The data can also identify which students were close to receiving high honors, being commended, or meeting mastery levels on state assessments.

When you get strategic with data, it helps you communicate immediate student needs. By combining your why with your immediate student needs, you can paint the destination your campus needs to reach.

Data can help illustrate a sense of urgency to disrupt the status quo. I have always found that data becomes relevant when you put names to the data. I didn't do this as a teacher, which was part of my failed data comprehension. As I moved into the administrative role, I witnessed great teachers own their data by knowing their kids.

James Barton, a Superintendent in Texas, brought data to life for his staff by displaying pictures of students during a faculty meeting. The images were shown for a variety of reasons, but the main point was: Do you know your kids?

I have seen outstanding teachers color code their seating charts by student needs. As teachers take attendance, they are reminded of which students they need to continue to monitor and question throughout the period. This is a straightforward way to remind teachers about who needs remediation during the period.

How can you, as the instructional leader, embrace owning data?

Data rooms or walls: Rooms or walls that display current student and teacher data. These rooms also provided a space to plan, describe, and debrief. This room is an excellent place to prepare and hold PLC meetings.

Data digs after assessments: A campus that owns its data has an effective PLC In place. Many successful educators gather after assessments to discuss their data. They analyze which question or standard scored lower than others, determining which concept or skill students experienced success in and which areas they fell short of. The discussion of data allows teachers to find bright spots in assessments and clone them.

Owning your data: If you were to ask your best teachers what skill or concept was missed the most on the last assessment, they would be able to tell you. Great teachers know which kids need a push, which need tutoring, and which will require small-group remediation. Jeff Vaughan, a long-time administrator in Texas, constantly challenged teachers with the following post-test strategy. He asked teachers to analyze the questions missed by the top students in the class. His theory was that if the top students missed a question, he didn't teach that concept. He would start the following day's lesson with the most missed questions by the top students.

When your mission disrupts the status quo, data should be utilized to create the urgency needed.

5. CONSTANTLY EXPLAIN WHY
This section could be titled, communicate, communicate, and then communicate some more. I have shared with you many times throughout *The Blueprint* that my lack of communication led to my rough start as a campus leader. With upfront and transparent

communication, teachers will know where you want to lead their campus. I like to think of teachers as sailors on a ship. They will gladly change direction if they know why.

When there is a lack of communication, misinformation fills in the gaps. When you fail to communicate why, anything – including gossip or resistance – can fill the void. As stated earlier, former Superintendent Dr. Alex Flores believes, "If you fail to communicate a why, one will be provided for you."

Looking back on my first year, I felt trapped in the belief that if I continued to discuss my why, teachers would get tired of it. From what I have learned, below-average teachers would have gotten tired of hearing my why, while the top teachers would have been cheering me on. Ten years into my principalship, I utilize every opportunity to communicate our core values and reiterate our mission statement. I celebrate every opportunity with our staff and community to ensure our course is charted.

> "The first step in that process is to develop a shared vision and mission. These cannot be statements that live on your campus website; they must be what you live by and that all believe in. We start every faculty meeting by reciting ours. As corny as that sounds, it has clarified what we are about and how we will operate as professionals. With that clarity comes the ability to reshape ineffective practices that do not align with the new mission and vision."
>
> Dr. Lance Groppel
> Deputy Superintendent of Administration
> Tyler ISD, Tyler, TX

He believes that this allows decision-making and discussions about change to be much more straightforward.

6. CREATE OPPORTUNITIES FOR YOUR STAFF TO GROW PROFESSIONALLY

I have found that change doesn't occur overnight. Here is how, using *The Blueprint,* you can begin to introduce effective instructional practices on campus.

To ensure that staff members were growing professionally, I took it upon myself to share educational articles with my staff about key instructional practices. It is one thing to say, "Todd Bloomer believes..." but another to say, "Noted author and educational leader Todd Whitaker supports..."

I am very active on social media. When I found an article that added value to our goals, I would tag teachers from my staff who were active on social media with the article. I would then follow up with teachers about the article, either electronically or in person. I would also select books for the staff to read that helped communicate my why. When I first became a principal, I wanted to mandate that all my department chairs participate in these book studies. However, as I evolved as a leader, I realized that I only wanted teachers who chose to be involved and so didn't require anyone to participate. By doing this, many of your instructional leadership team members will want to participate in the process. If an individual does not, you must ask if that person is the right person to lead that department.

Post-COVID, we highlighted the number of hours an educator worked outside the instructional day. Teachers work 15-20 hours outside their contract hours, and administrators at the high school level work 25-30 extra hours a week. This is a real dilemma for educators. How can we honestly hold teachers accountable for learning new practices independently?

I am very proud that our campus leadership team has committed to ensuring teachers grow professionally during the school day. In Silicon Valley, companies allow employees to improve their craft while on company time. At Apple, employees who want to work on projects can work on teams outside their specialization. Then there is Google's 20% time policy, which has begun to trickle into schools across America. Google has a philosophy they utilize that allows for employees to work on passion projects that could be outside their job description. The policy is called Google 20% Time. While working for Google, employees are allowed to spend time "on the clock" working on projects that interest them. This philosophy has started to enter schools around the country.

Would we ever allow this at a school? Would we allow a paraprofessional to work on a campus improvement project during the day? Should we allow teachers to work during the day on a project that was entirely outside their job description?

Our job as leaders on campus is to develop opportunities for our staff members to continue to grow. I challenge you to stretch your mind when allowing your staff to improve their craft.

7. HIRE PURPOSEFULLY AND HIRE FOR CHANGE

As a campus principal, our top priority is ensuring we have a great teacher in every classroom. Hiring is crucial when attempting to change the status quo. Focus on hiring teachers who can grow students academically. The most vital intervention for all students is high-quality initial instruction.

While I was the principal of Bradley Middle School, our leadership team supported a student-centered classroom. This meant that every teacher we hired needed to utilize their time with students to meet their needs. When hiring, our questioning was designed around their knowledge of a strong professional learning community.

If we consider the questions that a strong PLC is built around, could these be our questions during a teacher interview?

1. What do we want the students to know and be able to do?
2. How will we know if they learned it?
3. What do we do if a student already knows the material?
4. What do we do for the students who do not know the material?

While attending small group tutoring sessions is crucial, is tutoring the only way a student can learn the material?

Great teachers know they must close the daily learning gap to close the achievement gap. Students must "win" academically each day. They can't fall further behind by leaving a classroom confused or unsure of what is expected of them. Educational leader Kelly Harmon believes in closing the daily learning gap by making sure a student does not leave a classroom confused or further behind than when they entered the classroom.

As a middle school principal, I found that to implement a station rotation approach, I needed to hire teachers who utilized this approach each day.

I stumbled upon this philosophy when I hired a teacher from an elementary school named Ali Hill. She had been at an elementary school for two years and wanted to move to middle school. I didn't realize how transformational she could be to our campus.

I hired Mrs. Jennifer Aguilar during the summer of 2020. She was the instructional-minded leader that our campus needed and was an incredible person who knew the content and curriculum and had the respect of the staff because of her work ethic. Mrs. Aguilar addressed every inequity she encountered. If she found an outdated practice, she questioned it. If she discovered instructional practices that didn't meet the needs of ALL students, she asked about it. I would joke that if she found a rock, she looked underneath it. If she didn't like what was under the rock, she addressed it. She was one of my best hires during my tenure.

Keep your instructional focus in mind when selecting candidates for hire.

8. THE TIME TO CHANGE IS WHEN YOU ARE ON TOP

James Kerr, the author of *Legacy*, highlights the All Blacks, the winnest rugby team in the world. The All Blacks have a unique culture and a fascinating belief about when change is needed within their organization.

Most believe that change happens when the plan of action isn't working. Most would argue that if something is working, leave it alone. The All Blacks believe that the time to change is when you are on top, and everything appears to be working. Let that sink in for a moment.

> *The time to change is when you are on top, not when you are forced to change to remain relevant.*

From 1996-2001, the New York Yankees spoiled lifelong fans by dominating baseball during this time. They won four World Series championships during this fantastic run. I came to expect and believe that the Yankees would be in contention to win the World Series each year. Why wouldn't I?

Well, the Yankees leadership team felt the same way. They rested on their laurels, made some questionable moves, and began a slide into mediocrity. It would be a long time until the Yankees returned to dominance, and some would argue they still haven't. The Yankees stayed the same, and their complacency prevented them from staying on top.

In education, we face the same dilemma. I have seen many schools that waited until it was too late to implement change. How can we prevent this? Dr. Groppel observes, "People will be looking at what you allow because that speaks louder than any words you can say.
"

Disrupting the Status Quo
A Teacher Swap

This idea had been in my head for a while. It solidified when I was channel surfing one evening. I stopped on the TV show Wife Swap. Have you seen it before? Families are "swapped" for a period of time. Often the families are from different backgrounds and socioeconomic points. The show usually ends with realizations, epiphanies, and changed perceptions of life. My idea came together right there on my couch.

What if a teacher was swapped from campus A to campus B? What if teachers experienced environments utterly different from their current assignment? How might the experiences change their views or shape their practices? Why would we even think about swapping places to help change the status quo?

Often, educators attend a conference or in-service and are inspired to take what is learned back to their campus. But then life happens. Teachers get sidetracked, they have questions they can't get an immediate answer to about what they learned at the training, and they tend to fall back into the same routine. Since the presenter is not on campus, it becomes hard to replicate what was learned. But what if the presenter or expert joined our campus for a while to help model, troubleshoot, and assist our teachers?

I visited a campus that was using technology to teach math. The students were able to learn at their own pace using videos that allowed for instant feedback and provided the opportunity for students to learn at their own speed. I was impressed. A few weeks later, I brought two teachers back to see the effectiveness of the techniques. One of the teachers had incorporated the concept in her math class. While she had growing pains with the process, she persevered. How much easier would it have been if one of those teachers were moved to my campus to help implement the program?

George Couros, the author of The Innovator's Mindset, believes, "We rarely create something different until we experience something different." If we swapped teachers from campus to campus, the cultural exchange of ideas would flow as never before. What if a high-level physics teacher was swapped to a campus struggling to build its physics department? The master teacher could spend a semester with them, mentor the staff, then return to their home campus at the end of the swap.

After the teacher returned to the home campus, the collaboration could continue. Professional development could be re-structured to include partnerships with teachers that had been swapped. Teachers would feel much more comfortable reaching out to a colleague if they have worked with them for a while. With the ability to video conference, the possibilities for continued growth are endless.

Now, you might be intrigued by the idea. But to pull this off, we would have to remove and address many roadblocks and obstacles. Teachers would be the first to have objections. Change is complicated and messy for everyone. Administrators would have to address teachers' concerns and uncertainties. To make this work, the program should start small, possibly with volunteers or lead teachers in the first group. Principals would also need to address HR issues, such as how teachers would be evaluated.

Sometimes, leaders must blow the box up completely to think outside the box. By swapping teachers, educational best practices would be shared within our district that would benefit every student. Master teachers would share their craft. Teachers with incredibly high test scores could bring their bags of tools to campuses needing help to meet specific standards.

I was lucky to begin my teaching career on a Title I campus. But after four years, I was burned out and needed a change. I was taking two steps forward and three steps back. I left the district and relocated to San Antonio. But if I hadn't relocated, I might have left the profession as many young teachers do.

Would the knowledge that teachers could be swapped to campuses of different socioeconomic status prevent teachers from leaving our profession within the first five years? Would it prevent burnout? Would it attract more teachers to work in high-needs areas if they knew they could be swapped to a different campus during their tenure? Would a break recharge teachers? Even the military rotates troops to keep them fresh.

At times, educators need to remember why they got into their profession. We all do. I am not judging anyone. We have all been guilty of complaining about the kids on our campuses, often failing to realize how good we have it.

If we swapped teachers to different campuses, we could put what matters into perspective. The swap would also give teachers unique perspectives on kids in various parts of the city. What works in one zip code might not work in another.

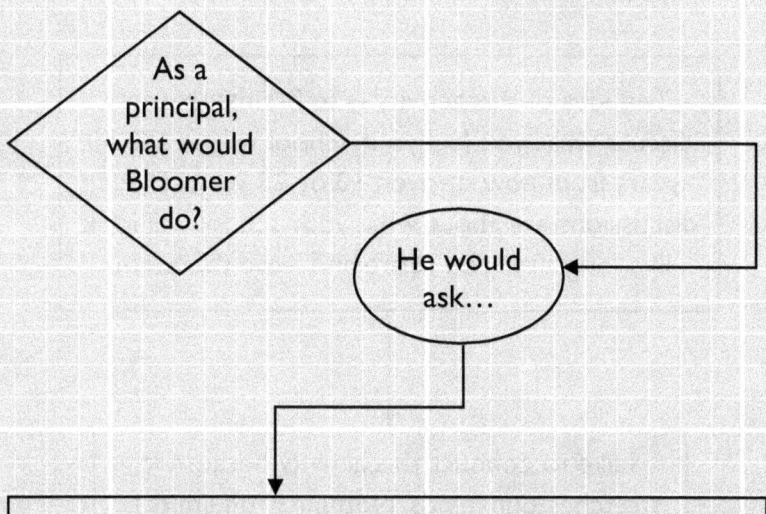

- How do you take a "temperature" reading of your staff to identify the status quo?
- How do you build consensus on your campus and battle the resistance?
- How do you ensure that your why is constantly at the forefront of your message to your staff and community?

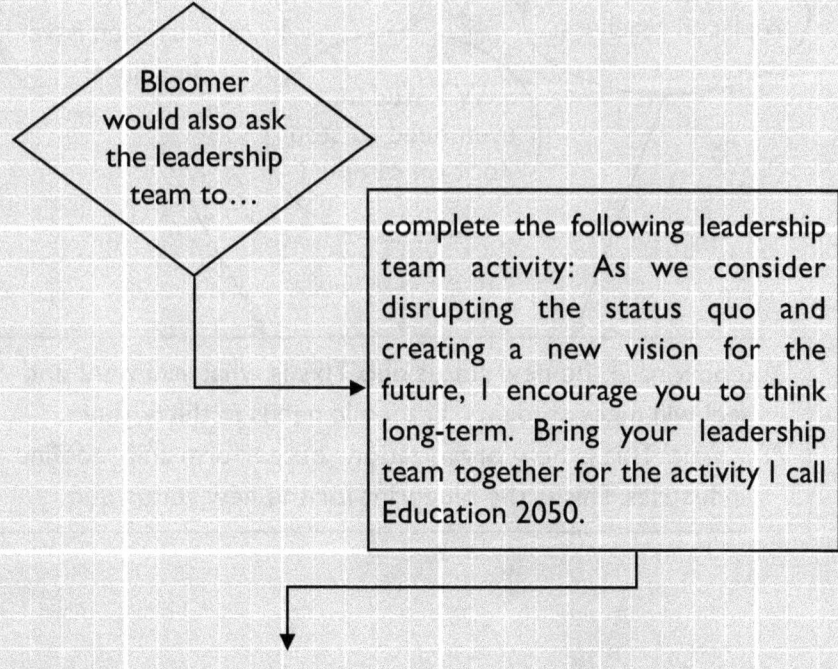

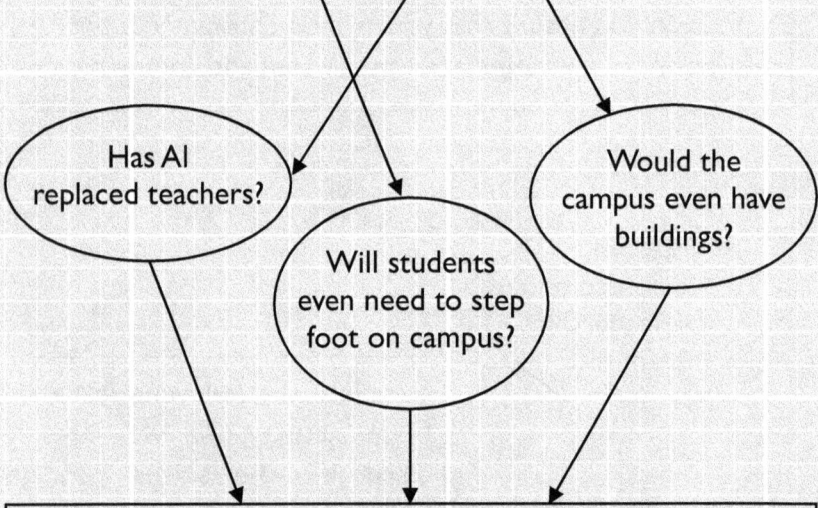

151

CHAPTER 5

Hiring—Doing the Work Up Front So You Don't Have to Work on the Back End

Ask members of your PLC to share their favorite interview questions with you as you prepare to hire teachers. I wouldn't just limit my quest to only educators. Frequently, corporations have great questions that allow them to find folks who are collaborative and problem solvers. Many of these corporations have developed outstanding questions that enable them to find specific candidates that fit their culture. Working within your PLN can help you build your questions to find the right candidate for the job.

True or False - Hiring is the most crucial aspect of your job. For a moment, think back to your preparation in graduate school for your role as an administrator. Think about the topics you discussed. What classes do you remember? What classes were beneficial to you? I never had a class on the hiring process. The longer I sat in my chair as the building principal, the more I realized that hiring was the most essential aspect of the job.

It is morally imperative that principals have an outstanding and loving teacher in every classroom across America. Long after you leave your job as the building principal, your legacy will be defined by the staff you leave behind to carry on the work. When I moved jobs, one of the hardest parts was leaving the teachers I had hired. They were my people, and they believed in our mission.

How much training have we received on interviewing and finding the best candidates for our school? Theory – yes, we received some training. Practical advice, questions, and solutions – no. The traditional hiring process involves posting the job, reviewing a resume, checking certifications, and calling the candidate for an interview. The interview questions were traditionally very superficial and didn't reveal much about candidates. During the process, we checked the references listed on the resume and made a decision, with the input of our committee. We then prayed that the desired results were what we needed. It was a crap shoot, and all too often, the process didn't get the results we desired.

Enter *The Blueprint*.

I will be honest; I like the hiring process. I am an educational headhunter. I chose the term headhunter because I believe that, as building principals, we should aggressively look for the best candidates for our schools.

Maybe you don't feel like you need to change your process. Why would you change what has been working in the past? Jennifer Gutierrez believes, "Hiring is vital; you either spend all of the time upfront to find the perfect fit for your campus or spend much time documenting later."

Jeremi Neifhoff, a colleague of mine and an administrator in my district, once shared the following story.

> *Mrs. Niefhoff asked a candidate she had just interviewed what the applicant had done to prepare for the interview. The candidate said nothing had been done to prepare. The candidate's brutal honesty made Mrs. Niefhoff ask why.*

The candidate shared something that cemented why we must ensure the hiring process changes. The candidate openly stated that all the questions they were asked in the interview process were variations of the same question. Once this candidate had attended one interview, they knew what to expect for the following interview.

Wow!

I applaud the candidate's bravery, but shame on us as administrators. We have become so comfortable and complacent that candidates don't need to prepare for an interview. Now, Mrs. Neihoff uses that same question with every candidate. I do as well.

These five principles allow me to find the best candidates possible:

1. Find someone you trust to vouch for the candidates.
2. Change the format of your interview process.
3. Find a candidate that fits your needs.
4. Don't be afraid to keep looking.
5. Remember, hiring is a year-round process.

1. FINE SOMEONE YOU TRUST TO VOUCH FOR THE CANDIDATES

Before anyone sits in front of my hiring committee, I have already vetted them to ensure they fit our campus culture and climate. The research phase is the most time-consuming part of the process, but it is also the key. As I review resumes and applicants, I note where they have worked, where they attended high school and college, and who they listed on their resume as references. I then start my research and call on my tribe for help.

Before anyone sits in front of my committee, I have already spoken to someone I can trust to who can verify the candidate has the qualities I am looking for. This is similar to the Six Degrees of Kevin

Bacon theory. You can always find someone who knows something about a candidate. On my team, assistant principal Jennifer Schaefer is that person. She grew up here, and everyone knew or went to school with her.

Houston, Texas-area administrator Crystal Romero-Mueller utilizes this approach during hiring: "I always call the references before the interview gets set up."

The question I use to get the most authentic beliefs about the potential candidate from their reference is, "If you opened a new campus, would you make this teacher first on the list of your new campus hires?"

I was recently interviewing for a counseling position, and many of the candidates were new or had worked in elementary schools previously. As a secondary school administrator, I didn't know many of the principals listed as references. Before I called the principals, I called a trusted elementary administrator. I wanted to hear from him whose opinion I could trust. I am not saying that your colleagues can't be trusted, but we all know that one administrator gives everyone stellar references regardless. It was this valuable insight that allowed me to pick a dynamic counselor.

What if you can't find someone to vouch for the candidate? The educational community is one of the most connected communities ever. While doing your research, I guarantee you can find a connection. Maybe your lead counselor worked at the school where an applicant is currently employed. This is a connection. You can ask the counselor to reach out to a trusted person. One of your department chairs may know a cooperating teacher with an outstanding first-year candidate applying for a position at your campus. This is a connection.

I have a friend who works in the largest district in San Antonio. If anyone from her district applies for a position on my campus, I contact her. She does some research and gives me an honest take. I do the same for her.

While I prefer to know the person giving out the information personally, sometimes I must rely on these connections before bringing someone to the committee.

Brian Buffini, a real estate and self-help millionaire, believes in this philosophy when hiring, "Can you put your name to it?" Can you look a friend or colleague in the eye and say you vouch for a candidate? Your word is your bond, and when making recommendations, you must take putting your name on a candidate extremely seriously. I only recommend someone who I would want to teach my children.

Sometimes, there are people on our campus that we hope leave the profession. They are hostile, burned out, or both. They make your job harder and are critical of everything you do. You can't eliminate them because they don't do enough to merit employee discipline. They have quietly quit teaching and are counting the days to retirement. When they apply for jobs, you celebrate. But, I would rather keep these teachers on my campus than put my name up as a recommendation. A problematic teacher is an issue for me, and I shouldn't pass the problem on to another school. Giving that person a strong reference is not morally or ethically right simply because you want them off your campus.

If you subscribe to the code of having to put your name to a candidate, you won't be able to recommend candidates that just don't cut it. How could you look at yourself in the mirror if you did?

2. CHANGE THE FORMAT OF YOUR INTERVIEW PROCESS

Every interview I conduct has the candidate teach a lesson to the committee. I make potential teachers, administrators, and counselors teach or present to the hiring committee. Having candidates teach a lesson to the committee will give you everything you need to determine whether this candidate is right for your position. You could end your interview after the teaching portion.

Here is how our interview process typically works:

Two days before the interview, I send the candidates the lesson objectives. I purposefully only give the candidates 48 hours because I want to see them in a time crunch. I also tell them they are only allowed a set time for the lesson.

I do this for two reasons. You can quickly tell if the candidate is a natural teacher. You should also see the candidates' A-game when delivering their content. If they can't engage me, they won't be able to command a classroom or staff meeting.

Where do I get the objectives for the lessons?

If a 6th-grade math position opens, I ask the best 6th-grade math teacher what lesson they would like to see the candidate teach to the committee. As I question the master teacher, I ask what questions that person would ask in the interview. Whenever possible, I have the department dean sit in on the interviews. Since I have already vetted the candidates, I give the department chair the final vote. The department leader must have a say in the teachers they work with.

I explain the process to the candidate as we begin the interview and give them five minutes to present to the committee. One committee member is tasked with keeping time. The candidates are also informed that the committee members will be part of an average classroom or meeting. While the candidate is teaching, you can quickly tell how confident the candidate is. How will they be with our students if they fumble through our presentation? After five minutes, we stop the candidate and give them a few moments to gather themselves. We then ask questions based on our lesson observations.

"I noticed that you used Google Slides to present the material. What other forms of technology are you comfortable using to present lessons?" or "I noticed that you didn't use technology to present your lesson to us; what forms of technology are you comfortable using in your classroom/job?" We follow up with questions such as, "How will you determine if your students mastered your objective for the lesson?" Based on how they respond, we follow up with questions to get to know the candidate.

I continue the questions with, "Say that you make an exit slip and find out more than half of the students don't grasp the objective; what would you do next?" We listen to their response and then keep prodding.

Another question I ask is, "You reteach and reassess and find that a group of students still fails to grasp the objective. What do you do with these students?" These students tend to be your ELL or SpEd students, and I want to hear the plan for those struggling all year. Will they pull small groups in class? Will they say they must move on because of scope and sequence?

I use the same process when interviewing counselors or assistant principals except their lesson tends to be a guidance or professional development topic on which they would lead the staff.

I would ask the assistant principal this question after their presentation:

During your presentation, a teacher in the crowd yells, "I love your passion and energy. The discussion was fun. But I tried this once, and it didn't work." How would you respond to this staff member?

If a counselor were interviewing for a position on my team, I would ask the candidate to conduct a small group guidance lesson for students. I would ask them what they would do if a student refuses to participate and asks to leave. I would then evaluate their answer.

How can a counselor work with a reluctant student and build relationships that would allow the student to open up to the counselor? Imagine the scenarios and questions you could ask candidates applying for a nurse's position or a librarian's position. We script the questions to ensure they are fair for all the candidates.

After we select a candidate, I keep a folder of what new hires answered for specific questions during the interview. If I ever need to talk to that teacher about issues ranging from high failure rates to negativity or students in general, I can reflect on our interview questions. "Remember our interview? Remember how you explained to the committee that you would do whatever it took to help your students succeed? Let's talk about…" While I have never had to follow up with teachers that I have hired by utilizing this elaborate process, I keep the notes in case that day arises.

You might be thinking, *I don't have time for this process. It will take forever!* I understand that. During my first summer as a high school principal, I hired almost 30 teachers. If I didn't have time to have them teach, I adapted to find the best candidate for the position. During the interview, I used role-playing. We were trying to lay the foundation for strong professional learning committees, and I wanted to see how the candidates would operate within a PLC. I had my committee members ask questions about a lesson they were developing and see how the candidate responded.

- "I have many ELL kids in my class; how would you recommend that I approach them?"
- "I want to incorporate student choice into this lesson. How have you utilized student choice in lessons previously?"
- "How can I incorporate technology?"

This allowed me to gain insight into their instructional tool bag.

I have also had athletic coaches role-play a parent meeting in which the parents were upset about their son's playing time. I created questions based on scenarios that would allow me insight into how the coach would respond.

In Texas, football is king. The head football coach is a critical and influential position. Why wouldn't you want to see them teach from the game film during an interview? I don't want to see the 80-yard touchdown run but the run that lost eight yards, and I have to teach the committee what went wrong. How many committees do this for head coaches?

During these role-playing sessions, you are able to dig in and see what you are interviewing for. These responses are not canned but tend to come from the heart.

Another question I like to ask revolves around a candidate's personal growth. One of my favorite questions is, "What is the last educational book you have read?" This question allows me to see if the candidates continue to read and grow in their profession. If the last book they read is a textbook from college or a testing manual, then the candidate might need to catch up with their growth.

I also put five books in front of the candidates such as Jimmy Casas' book *Culturize* or Darrin Peppard's *Road to Awesome*. I ask them if they have read any. These are books I have read or my staff has read for a book study. They are also books that I have discussed on social media. This gives me an idea of who wants to work for me and follows me on social media. In researching a potential job, I think you would review the principal's social media footprint. I like to watch the candidates review the books and, if they have not read them, explain to me which one they would like to read and why.

> " *I am changing the interview game because I want to find candidates to change the game for our students.* "

As you develop questions for your interview process, I recommend crafting questions about your campus needs. If your campus is implementing professional learning communities, craft a question to determine their familiarization and knowledge of professional learning communities. If your campus struggles with gossip or empathy or has a high-performing culture, focus on developing questions that allow insight into these areas.

A teacher approached me and said current teachers heard about the new interview process and didn't like it. I laughed and then asked why. She explained there was too much pressure on teachers and why wouldn't I just do a traditional interview. I laughed, shrugged, and wished I could have used the interview process on this teacher because I wouldn't have hired her. The process would have revealed that someone other than this person was the right fit for advancing the course we were charting. It probably wouldn't be a shock to you that this teacher was struggling with changing demographics and a changing student body would it?

I have utilized this process over fifty times in the last five years. I only have one teacher that got past us with this system. That is a pretty good track record for the interview process.

Take time on the front end to ensure you have the best teachers working in your school buildings. The hiring process is one of the most critical aspects of an administrator's job.

> *"We go with the candidate's heart first. We can teach the skills necessary to be a great teacher, but changing an individual's heart/mindset is much harder. We develop questions to help gain insight into a candidate's perspective during the interviewing process."*
>
> *Stacy Kimbriel*
> *Elementary Principal, School, Plano, TX*

What is next?

Dr. Melissa Acala, principal of the CAST Tech High School within the San Antonio Independent School District, has added another piece to the interview process: She pre-screens candidates for an interview on her campus. Dr. Alcala and her committee review the applicants who apply for a position. Those who make their first round of cuts are emailed and asked to submit a video to the committee answering a specific question. This screening process allows Dr. Alcala to review a larger pool of candidates. Only some people who submit a video are granted an interview.

In the summer of 2019, I was hiring for an assistant principal position. I utilized a video component to screen candidates. I sent nine candidates an open-ended question and asked them to make a two-minute video of their responses. From the nine I sent the question to, I interviewed five candidates. I was so pleased with the results of the video question that I continued to utilize Dr. Alcala's approach.

Student panels

I also utilize student panels to help make critical hiring decisions. I select students representing our student body and have them brainstorm questions they want to ask candidates. I am transparent with the students up front. I need honest feedback and confidentiality maintained. I have never had an issue with this because the students appreciate the opportunity to have a voice on their campus. I also clearly articulate that they have a voice, not a vote, to ensure I comply with our Human Resources Department.

I don't tell the candidates they are meeting with a student panel. We just build it into their allocated time and walk them straight into a room with students. The candidate is asked a series of questions by the students, then brought to the "normal part" of the interview with the staff members. The candidates say the student panel was the most enjoyable and challenging part of the interview. Kids can spot authenticity a mile away. With each student panel I convened, the students' choice of candidate was the same as ours.

Student ownership of a school is a vital component of the Triangle of Success. When selecting a Band Director or Dance Team coach, including student voice goes a long way with the students and their parents. It also signals to the candidate that I value students' voices and expect them to do the same.

3. FIND A CANDIDATE THAT FITS YOUR NEEDS

This seems like a no-brainer, but doing the work upfront is vital. I review each candidate's resume when they apply. I look for certifications, experience, and objectives/qualifications. Many districts have certification officers to help determine if a candidate is qualified for a position. I have learned that just because a candidate applied doesn't mean the person can teach that subject. I have also learned the hard way that bringing in candidates who are not qualified wastes everyone's time.

As the hiring manager of my campus, I have learned when and why alternative certification candidates can be considered for a position. These requirements need to be clarified. Taking time to vet and ensure the candidate has the proper certification for the position is imperative. Like proper certification, evaluating the importance of experience presents a challenge. Middle School Principal Cynthia Rubio believes, "You hire the right person for the campus, not necessarily the person with the most experience."

As a high school principal, I sit in every interview. This is extremely time-consuming but necessary to help me ensure that we bring the right people to the family. "I look for people who have a sense of community, who are positive, who seem to love being around children, who can provide something to a team that is lacking," said Marty Silverman, Retired Principal from the San Antonio-area.

During the selection process, I look for resumes that stand out from traditional ones. I have seen candidates use QR codes to link their resumes to their websites or social media feeds. I will honestly say that any resume with a QR code will receive more attention than a traditional resume. I look for teachers who have a strong technology background because this is an area that I believe will help us change instructionally.

I have seen candidates list their social media digital footprint. This practice allows me to gain a perspective on the candidate's philosophy and beliefs. I believe that having a strong professional social media footprint indicates that a candidate is a lifelong learner and open to new ideas. I firmly believe in lifelong learning, and I have found that those with an active digital footprint tend to fall into that category.

I then look for a candidate's qualifications or skills that they can bring to the campus. Are they willing to be athletics coaches? Do they want to sponsor a club? Were they a former cheerleader? We all know that we are constantly looking for coaches and sponsors.

I also look for the technical skills they list as competent in. I never want to see another resume that lists teachers fluent in Microsoft

PowerPoint or Microsoft Word. I want to see teachers who list their technology qualifications as Nearpod or Mentimeter.

From this original vetting, I develop a list of possible candidates based on qualifications to be considered for employment. I then take the names and run them through every social media channel I know. I don't want any surprises.

NFL star Josh Allen of the Buffalo Bills had embarrassing tweets resurface from when he was in high school. Did anyone in the Bills organization find these tweets before he was drafted? Major League Baseball player and 2018 All-Star Josh Hadder had a similar incident. While both incidents occurred in their teenage years, someone should have found these embarrassments.

If your social media account shows your trips to the bars, your vacation in the Caribbean, and your profanity directed toward political leaders, I don't want you on my campus.

With a positive social media presence, you are at the top of my list for an interview. Without a social media presence, I question your personal growth, and if everything is equal, I might not interview you.

When I became the principal of Churchill High School, I urged my staff to follow me on Twitter so they would know where I stood on any important topic.

Last, even though I have the final say in recommendations, I rely on my team to provide valuable advice. My instructional leadership team comprises the science, English, social studies, and math department's instructional leaders.

During a recent interview, I shared with the instructional leadership team that my vote would be what they felt was suitable for our school—being able to rely on Ginger McDaniel, Lesley Knife,

Meridith Birdy, and Kathleen Janysek and support their decision allowed for an effective work environment. Through hard work, we have developed a rapport and trust that allows us to have honest conversations. With this healthy relationship, we have continued to build something special.

Doing your homework is crucial in ensuring you get the best candidates for the position you are searching for.

4. DON'T BE AFRAID TO KEEP LOOKING

Never settle for a candidate that doesn't fit your vision or campus. I don't care what time of the year you are hiring; don't ever be afraid to keep looking. When you settle on a candidate, the long-term ramifications could be disastrous. Your students deserve the best, even if that means going with a long-term substitute teacher until you can find the right fit for your campus. I have never had difficulty explaining to parents that I couldn't settle on a candidate because their child deserved better.

Author and former principal Adam Dovico also asserts, "Hiring is one of my most important elements to moving my school forward. The people in the building make a difference, so I need the best. I will conduct dozens of interviews until I find the right person for the job. I cannot settle on a person for convenience. I am looking for people who already fit into the culture I have built. I am not hiring people who cannot keep up with our high-energy, fast-paced culture. Luckily, as word has gotten out about our school, I am now attracting candidates who already fit the mold."

The building principal and committee selecting candidates should always be on the same page about the campus needs and goals of the interview process. If you don't have a consensus, take time before the interviews begin to discuss the needs. Guide the discussion to the qualities and characteristics you seek in this position.

As the principal, you are always in charge of the interview process. While I have never been a dictator in this process, I am the final hiring decision-maker. The committee knows that my vote counts more than the others.

> "Do not put too many people on your interview committee. Too many opinions can make the process confusing. With big positions — ask the committee to give you the top two names, and don't be afraid to call for a second interview."
>
> Cynthia Rubio
> Principal, San Antonio, TX

While I have never had to override the committee's decision, I reserve that right. This is because we are all on the same page before we begin the interviews. Once I am ready to offer a candidate a position on campus, I take a few moments and lay out my expectations. Remember, clear is kind, and I want to ensure we are on the same page.

Here are the following points I touch on:
1. I expect all teachers to put kids first, but I say, "I need you to put yourself first and take care of yourself so that you can put kids first."
2. I expect fierce loyalty to our campus, and I know that teaching is a very challenging profession. I expect positivity on social media, in meetings, and with colleagues. I say, "Ain't nobody got time for negativity." I also make it a point to say that I don't want to see any Facebook posts blaming kids or pointing out something negative about our campus or community.
3. I expect all teachers to work to be the best that they can be. All teachers will attend meetings, participate actively, and

work to improve daily. I only micro-manage teachers who need it and will treat them like the professionals they are!
4. I expect all teachers never to blame students, parents, or our zip code. I tell them, "So what, now what?" and expect them to have the same philosophy.
5. I expect all teachers to get involved and attend games, concerts, school plays, and other activities we have on campus.
6. I will need each teacher at least one Saturday during the year, and will pay them to help prepare for state exams. I do this because I will need them and often have had to remind folks of what they said before they accepted my offer.
7. I end by sharing that I live 1.2 miles from campus, and this community means a lot to me. All five of my children graduated from our school, and I am with our students and parents when I go grocery shopping or to mass. Because of that, I am passionately driven to make our community everything it needs to be.

While it is a lot, it is essential to share this with candidates. I then ask for a commitment. Are they willing to change the game for our students and community? If so, I welcome them aboard. If not, I keep looking.

5. REMEMBER: HIRING IS A YEAR-ROUND PROCESS

This has to become your philosophy for acquiring great talent. This mindset has allowed me to find and hire amazing candidates when positions open on my campus. Here is where we truly become headhunters.

I often joke with my administrative team that I have a "guy" or a "lady" when a position opens on campus. I have an "ace in the hole" because I do the leg work year-round in acquiring talent.

This was on display when I hired Tamara Marler, a long-time Special Education Coordinator in our district. I had spoken with her throughout the years, and when she was ready, we made it happen. She is an excellent assistant principal at Churchill High School.

Every interaction with every educator is a potential job interview. They might not know this, but I am constantly looking to acquire the best talent for my team. I am building a Golden State Warriors-type team by acquiring all-stars at every teaching position.

> "Most importantly, we are now more aggressive with our recruiting. We take note of strong people we meet at conferences, ceremonies, and events, and we personally cold call them and invite them to interview,"
>
> Shane Mckay
> Former Principal,
> East Central ISD, San Antonio, TX

Here are the places where I typically search for candidates throughout the year.

Social media

As I have said, teachers must have an active social media presence. I have had the tremendous opportunity to connect with outstanding educators through social media. If you have yet to be active on social media (who are you?), let me spell out another significant benefit.

When the committee interviews candidates, we often wish we knew where they stood on multiple issues. Twitter and LinkedIn allow you to see the educational philosophy of every potential candidate. With a bit of research, you can determine if candidates fit the needs of your campus. I have found and connected with many educators I have hired or actively recruited to join my campus.

Conferences are job interviews
I love to attend conferences for many reasons. I love being able to network and collaborate with colleagues. But now, I look at conferences as a place to find teachers and administrators to join my team. I always carry my business cards with me wherever I go. When I see a teacher or administrator I can envision working on my campus, I approach them after the presentation. I congratulate them and say, "If you are ever looking for a change, let me know."

I presented at the La Cosecha Conference in Santa Fe, New Mexico, in November 2018. This is the largest dual-language conference in America. When I met teachers, I handed them my card to let them know I would talk with them if they wanted to relocate to San Antonio, Texas.

Create a school where people want to work
How can you find the best talent? How can you get people to send you their resumes and express an interest in joining your team? Create a place where educators want to work, and candidates will knock on your door. I equate this to the movie *Field of Dreams,* "If you build it, they will come."

I have found that people want to be a part of something special. Doesn't everyone want to be on a winning team? Again, the Golden State Warriors are a prime example of superstars wanting to be a part of something special. The same can be said for educators.

Our mentality is that we are building something special on our campus and are fearless in telling people about it. My job is to generate the excitement and fuel that propels the engine forward. I am creating a campus that empowers teachers, celebrates students, and embraces the community. Who wouldn't want to be a part of this?

"We are chasing championships!" This is one of my favorite sayings, and it describes almost anything we do! I am blessed to work with exceptional instructional deans who lead our campus. I have challenged them to help recruit the teachers they want in their department. This helps me and allows our leaders to build their departments.

In the summer of 2022, my science dean, Mrs. Karin Montemayor, brought me three teachers who fit our campus culture, and we hired them all. If she liked them, I wanted them. I had the utmost trust in my extended leadership team.

I use social media to create a buzz around my campus. I constantly share positive tweets about my staff, student body, and community. I made the persona of the Bradley Nation and the Churchill Nation to describe my school. I used hashtags like #allinall4bradley and #bettertogether to generate excitement. I talked constantly about how I empowered my teachers, how my students created, and how my community supported them.

Everyone wants to be a part of something special. By sharing a glimpse into our school life, I can entice other staff members to want to join the family. Little did I know that when I started tweeting in 2010, the little blue bird would help me find the best candidates for my campus.

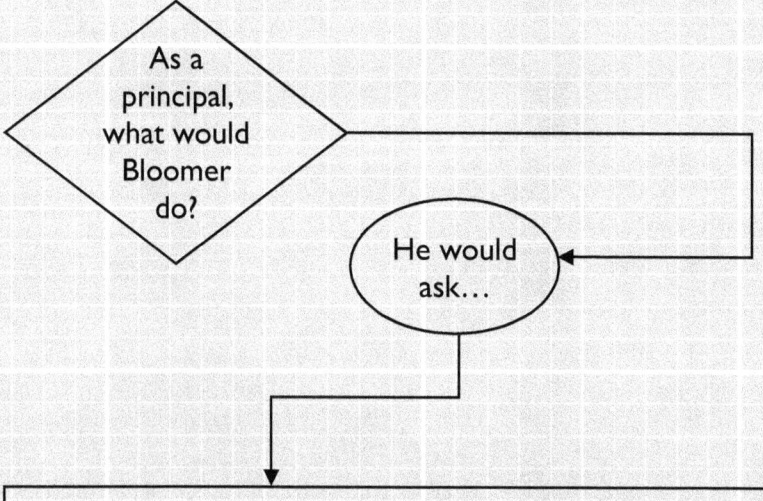

- As a leader, do you have the right people in your school and in the right spots? If not, what is your plan?
- How do you create a school where teachers and support staff want to work for you?
- What questions do you ask during your interviews that help you find the best candidates for your campus?
- What questions can you eliminate that don't assist you in accomplishing the goal of finding the best candidates?

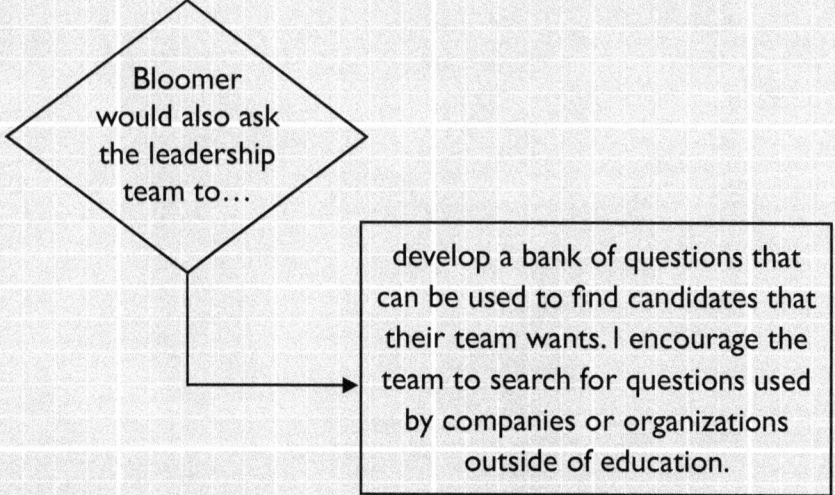

CHAPTER 6
Managing Your Time So It Doesn't Manage You—The Blueprint to Developing a Work Balance for You

The Blueprint encourages leaders to utilize podcasts to expand their leadership skills. I have replaced music on my walks or long commutes with podcasts. They have helped me grow professionally and balance my work and life.

For me, a typical day begins before sunrise and often ends after sunset. It's not uncommon for me to repeat this schedule multiple times throughout the week. Not many jobs emulate that of a principal. In most places of employment, you can make a to-do list in the morning and expect to accomplish most of it by the end of the day. With the principal's job, to-do lists can be tossed out the window with one phone call or one student or parent concern.

During my first tenure as an assistant principal, I used to joke that if I could make it through the waiting area in the front office when I arrived without having a parent waiting for me, it would be a good day! I say this facetiously, but it clearly illustrates my point. We are on the job from the moment we wake up until we fall asleep.

As a first-year administrator, I didn't have a time management system. I was in reaction mode all the time and surviving day to day. I was genuinely playing the whack-a-mole game. I was putting out fires (literally) in restrooms, disciplining students, returning parent calls, monitoring passing periods, and supervising lunch duty. I wonder if teachers could see me just spinning out of control.

I wish to travel back in time to advise and support a younger first-year administrator, Todd Bloomer. The blueprint was created and designed for just that need. I wish I had realized during my first year the importance of routines, schedules, and effective time management. It is incredible that I even survived my first few years when I reflect on them.

The saying "When everything is important, then nothing is" is true. This is common for many first-year administrators. They don't realize what is essential and fail to manage their time. They put the same energy and time into every issue – the failure to prioritize leads to frustration, missing deadlines, and confusion.

I now have a system that works for me. I will share the blueprint for time management with you in this chapter. Here is my checklist:

1. Put kids first. Wait…
2. Find a system that works for you.
3. Find joy during the day.

1. DON'T PUT KIDS FIRST – PUT YOURSELF FIRST

This statement goes against everything I believe in. We have always been told to put kids first, haven't we? While I still practice this, if we do not put ourselves first, then what we do doesn't matter because we will struggle in everything we do.

The first system you need to establish is a system for you! Without a strong you, nothing else matters. Your mental and physical well-being is the first system you must establish. Make sure that you take care of yourself!!

One of the first things we often neglect when we become administrators is ourselves. Our extended hours frequently lead to unhealthy eating. When our routines involve grabbing fast food on the way home, we all know what is subsequent – weight gain. Long hours and fried foods tend to disrupt our health. We can all say that this will not happen to us, but it does.

Author and speaker Jimmy Casas encourages all administrators to give 2% of their day back to themselves. Two percent of your day is 30 minutes. He encourages us to exercise— walk, run, try yoga, or lift weights for at least that amount of time.

A movement on Twitter has evolved, #fitleaders. The postings address the direct neglect of ourselves and our health. Adam Welcome wrote a book titled Run Like a Pirate about our health. In El Paso, Texas, Principal Charlie Garcia uses #lifefit with his staff and colleagues. By modeling his system for self-care, he has inspired others to take care of themselves.

Many educators work out before or after work. They realize the importance of taking care of themselves. Often, we give so much of ourselves that we don't have anything left in our bucket. Tina Lozano models self-care better than anyone I know. She runs each morning, and running over 100 miles a month is not uncommon. She also serves as a high school assistant principal. More importantly, she challenges me to continue to run. From gentle prodding to downright calling me out, we all need someone to hold us accountable to exercise more.

We can't give from an empty bucket! If you look at me, I am not a picture of health. I fell victim to the hours and sacrificed my well-being to ensure everyone else was cared for. When I got home, I sat on the couch and watched TV instead of lacing up my shoes and going for a walk or a run most nights. I might have mixed in an adult beverage, which soon became my routine.

As I became a high school administrator, the stress of the job was more than I had expected. I realized that one of three things was going to occur. I was going to start working out, I was going to allow the stress of the job to force me onto medication, or I was going to become an alcoholic. I don't say the last two lightly.

I dedicated myself to working on my health. I make it a priority to get at least thirty minutes of exercise each day. I decided to make this a routine and not just a goal. If I could make this a habit, the system of working on my mental and physical health would be solid.

Rogers High School Principal Dr. Lee Vi Moses runs five miles every Wednesday evening. He does this while his children are at gymnastics. This routine allows Dr. Moses to stay in great physical shape.

San Antonio Principal Cynthia Rubio is an avid runner. She runs with her leadership team, and that strengthens their bond. Not only is she in excellent physical condition, but you can also find her running with her school's cross-country team. Parents see this, and students love it.

> "Running allows me to engage with adults outside my professional life, and it still holds me accountable for things like training, goal setting, celebrating milestones, and putting in hard work and dedication. My mindset and work ethic toward my wellness is similar to the effort I put into my job. I want to be intentional about my efforts; otherwise, there will be no improvement."
>
> Cynthia Rubio
> Principal, San Antonio, TX

> "When you continually take in information that is either sensitive or toxic, and you don't have a place to deposit it, it will lead to decreased mental health." He continues, "I

would reconsider the goal to amass hundreds of sick days. Tomorrow is neither guaranteed nor promised."

Melvin Echard
Principal, San Antonio, TX

During COVID, I found myself in my doctor's office, worried I had acquired the virus. My doctor prescribed me Xanax. He could see the stress in my mind and around my midsection. He told me that I needed to get out and exercise. He was worried about me, and my wife was also concerned about me. I realized that if I didn't care for myself, none of the hard work or systems I hoped to implement would matter. One of my colleagues has a saying that helps drive home the point of putting yourself first. "If we died on the job, they would name a replacement before we were put in the ground."

Let that sink in as you read the rest of this chapter.

How am I trying to take care of myself?
- I get plenty of sleep. I try to be in bed each night by 9 pm. Some days, I sleep until 7 am and still make it to work before most.
- I make exercise a priority. I work out six days a week now. This is important.
- I have mentally given myself permission not to attend every event our school participates in or be the first to work or last to leave.

Balancing work and family

How many of you have uttered this statement before? We need to find a balance. But let's ask ourselves this question: Is there ever a true balance? Are we trying to attain something that isn't attainable? We never seem to find a balance. Instead, we need to be honest about examining our personal lives. When you are with your spouse, be there with your spouse. Be there not just physically but in mind and spirit. Be attentive. When you are eating dinner with your family, be there. *When home, be home.*

At one point, I experienced a rough patch at work. My superintendent, Dr. Sean Maika, contacted me to check in. After thanking him, I told him that my wife and I were going out to dinner and I was leaving my cell phone at home. You know what? The school didn't fall, nobody needed me, and my wife and I enjoyed an excellent meal.

Churchill Mental Health Counselor, Mrs. Kathy Johnson, ensures that the adults she works with make their mental health a priority. From check-ins to a joyous smile, she realizes that adults must be at their best to do their job.

After I hired a new football coach on campus, Mrs. Johnson realized that I had taken criticism from stakeholders who supported another candidate. She could tell it was wearing on me. She closed my door one morning just to check in on me. We all need a Kathy Johnson, and I am lucky that the Churchill community has the original.

My wife and I have incorporated Five Good Minutes into our evenings. We dedicate five minutes to each other to talk about our day. We turn off the TV and phones and just talk. Typically, this is the highlight of my day and lasts for much longer than five minutes.

Coach Tim Woods has been married for over 25 years and shares his one job with me when his wife gets home. They are both educators, and his wife, Kim Woods, has taught for 30 years at the same middle school. Tim's job is to sit on the couch, listen to his wife talk about her day, and keep her from being on the sofa's edge.

But being present is much more complicated than it sounds. I have seen the principal job swallow up the best of people and divide families and marriages.

This section is hard to write because I have been fortunate to have a wonderful and understanding partner throughout my journey. My wife, Sharon, has allowed me to put my career ahead of her aspirations. Sadly, I might have sometimes put my career ahead of our family. I am not proud to admit that I have missed family engagements for my job. I am not proud to admit it, but I have missed my children's events for the job.

In my first year as a principal, I felt I needed to attend every event my school had. I wanted my community to see that I was all in. Many of us would read this statement and shake our heads in agreement. But this came at the expense of my son Andrew. He went to a different school in our district, and when he was in seventh grade, his football games were on the same day as our games. I missed almost all his football games that year to attend my school's games. A student's parent at my school approached me at a football game. She asked me why I wasn't watching his game. I told her that I needed to be at my school's games. She looked at me and said, "Every parent here would want you at your son's game if they knew you were missing it to be here!"

Entrepreneur Tim Denning believes, "The greatest workplace perk is being on time to have dinner with your family each night." As I have evolved as a leader, I have come to understand that to have a strong family life, I need to be present in the moment. When at home, I needed to be present. When at work, I needed to be present there.

Author Adam Grant believes, "Too many people wait until they're exhausted or depressed to make a change or seek help. Mental health isn't something to put on the back burner. We can't keep good habits in storage until we need them. Mental hygiene should be as ingrained in our daily routine as dental hygiene."

"When you go home, be with your family. Take email off of your phone. I believe that there is no such thing as an emergency email. People should and need to have your phone number."

Dr. Lance Groppel
Deputy Superintendent of Administration
Tyler ISD, Tyler, TX

You know that I am a Twitter guy. I credit Twitter with propelling my career. I have made many long-lasting professional friendships and relationships because of the little blue bird. I have hosted Twitter chats, and I actively participate in them. I enjoy the connections and appreciate the fraternity I am a part of because of Twitter.
But I had to change my routine when I arrived home to be more present. My wife and kids would say I am still working on them.

- Once you get home, do something immediately with your spouse and children. This can be as simple as taking a walk or playing a game.
- Put your phone in a location that makes monitoring inconvenient.
- Designate a time at home dedicated to school work and stick to that time.
- Schedule time for social media and ensure it doesn't interfere with your family time.

These small changes in my routine when I arrive home allow me to be more present with my family. Family members deserve your attention when you are home.

Take care of your spouse
As mentioned earlier, having a willing partner is critical to your success. Your partner needs to be treated like the king or queen they are. As you develop a successful work and family balance, you

must ensure that time is always spent with your spouse. I have seen this job destroy marriages.

My wife and I are blessed to live in a beautiful city. San Antonio is filled with diverse food and music. We enjoy finding new places to eat on our nights out. The key is that we dedicate time to being together. We developed a Sunday routine of walking in our city together. We try to find a new place to have a snack at the end of our walk. This fun outing allows us to spend time together, exercise, and explore new restaurants. We look forward to the time together. We don't miss a Sunday Funday!
Make your spouse realize their importance to your success. Don't forget them.

2. FIND A SYSTEM THAT WORKS FOR YOU

This might seem simple, but I can't stress enough the importance of finding a time management system. As a principal, I have found a system that works for me, but it took time and trial and error. The key is that I found a system that works. Here are some standard practices and traits that successful educators utilize.

Arrive early or stay late - don't do both

I am an early bird. I like to wake up by 5:30 am each day. I have started reading scriptures in the morning to help focus and centralize my day. Many colleagues start their day reading, praying, or meditating. This routine allows me to start my day successfully and in a positive mental place. Some mornings, I will go for a run or hit the gym before going to work. I arrive at school by 7:30 am and begin to prepare for work. I have found that arriving before the students and most adults arrive allows me to get the most done. I review my calendar for the day, write thank you notes, and set up my Recharge Zone. While I can only partially lay out my day, I develop a schedule of what I would like to accomplish if everything goes well.

It's all about systems

I was never going to let a colleague outwork me. As a principal, I wanted to model for my assistants the time and effort it took to get the job done. As an assistant principal, nobody needed to tell me the job wasn't from 8:00 am to 4:00 pm.

If I could travel back in time and talk with first-year administrator Todd Bloomer, I would help him develop systems and structures to manage his day. Most early administrators don't have a system, and that is evident. The most straightforward system is utilizing your calendar to drive your activities. I now put everything on my calendar and have found that my tasks actually get done!

On Monday, I block my calendar from all meetings to be in classrooms. My secretary knows classroom observations are essential to me and something only gets scheduled on that day if it is an emergency. On Tuesday, I schedule time to start writing my community newsletter. First-year principal Todd Bloomer waited until Friday to write and send it out. I only spend 15 minutes on it now, but that is significant. Also, on Tuesday, I write five thank you notes to staff members who live our Winston Churchill Mission and Vision.

On Wednesday, my calendar has me spending another 15 minutes on my newsletter and 15 minutes writing emails to all staff members, the student body, and new teachers. I used to delay delivering these messages, waiting until the last minute to send them. The quality is much better when scheduling a few minutes daily to work on them. I also schedule time for coffee with my lead counselor and athletic director. You would be surprised how important and beneficial these meetings are.

On Thursday, I schedule time to continue finalizing my communications. The student email goes out Friday at 5:30, and the parent newsletter goes out Friday at 5 pm. My secretary also has time now to proofread my work.

On Friday, I schedule time to review grade books. While I do not enjoy this part of the job, it helps me avoid issues or concerns. I also schedule time to monitor student attendance and grades as well as make parent calls on Friday. Last, I have time to finalize my staff emails and schedule their delivery for Monday mornings. By developing these structures, I don't have to come to work Sunday mornings to get these emails out. I calendar what is essential to me.

I am blessed to work with Assistant Principal Anthony Allen. He utilizes his calendar to drive his day. Anthony has found that if he does not add it to his calendar for the day, it probably doesn't get done. As an assistant principal in charge of discipline and attendance, he has learned the importance of his calendar.

Prioritize what needs to get done that day

Prioritizing what needs to be accomplished during your day is essential in managing the day. If your boss needs a report to be done, and the deadline is that morning, then that task would be something to be completed immediately. If you have a parent coming in to meet with you regarding an important issue or concern, that would take precedence that morning. If a teacher asked to speak with you during her conference, that meeting would be at the top of the list. Once you have generated your list, prioritize when the following tasks will be done:

When will you visit with students regarding attendance or discipline?
When will you visit classrooms?
When do you have to monitor lunch duty?
Are there parents that you need to return calls to?
All administrators know that being visible is necessary to be successful.

If you do not plan well, you can see why many administrators get trapped in their offices. Successful administrators have systems that help manage their days. Inexperienced administrators let the day run them.

When I see administrators sitting at their offices or desks for long periods, I ask what they are working on. If I have time, I ask them to walk with me and visit a classroom. Every Monday afternoon, I invite an administrator to walk with me for an hour. During this time, I have the administrator select classrooms to visit. Walking with them, we can calibrate what we see after leaving the room. We always follow up with teachers after our visits.

During the second hour of my visit with the administrator, we can do one of two things: continue visiting classrooms or talk about anything on their minds. We may discuss projects and plans that they are in charge of. This private time allows us to grow closer as a team, and I look forward to it.

Having an accountability partner is central to motivating each other to visit classrooms

If you have partners as assistant principals, I would challenge them to see who could do the most observations each week. I would also walk by their office and encourage them to walk classrooms together. If you are the only assistant principal, I would challenge the principal to these same walks.

I have established a monthly group of high school principals who walk campuses and share feedback. While it originally started as a way to help monitor classroom instruction, the outsider eyes on the campus have helped with school safety and student flow patterns. This costs nothing except some time out of my day. I highly recommend a system like this to assist you.

How I manage to stay on top of work email

Email can dominate your day and pull you in many different directions. Checking and staying on top of work email is essential, But there should be a time and place to read and answer them. I encourage my administrative team to monitor their email and respond timely. While the 24-hour rule is common when returning emails or calls, this is cold, and parents and teachers need a response much sooner. Try to consistently answer emails or phone messages before leaving work.

> "I trust and allow my administrative assistant to read my email and address concerns. When I open my email, I know that everything unread needs my attention and that I am not wasting my time reading things."
>
> Dr. Lance Groppel
> Deputy Superintendent of Administration
> Tyler ISD, Tyler, TX

With smartphones, email can be synced to our phones and answered from any location. This remarkable convenience allows you to answer emails from the grocery store or the comfort of your couch. (I had to remove email from my iPhone during my tenure because I became a servant to my phone. If it pinged with a notification that I had received an email, I checked, answered, or stressed.)

> "There is no such thing as an emergency email. People should have your cell phone number for emergencies."
>
> Dr. Bobby Martinez
> Assistant Superintendent of Secondary Education,
> Alvin, TX

As a middle school principal, I removed email from my phone, which was one of my most liberating moves. I needed this piece of mind to manage my time personally. I knew that if a central office member had a serious concern, they would call or text me. If they emailed me, I could respond to it the following day. During my 5 am routine, I would check my email from the time I left work the previous day and be able to respond at that time. This worked for me.

As a high school principal, I have email back on my phone. But I delete it over significant holidays and communicate to my community that I am unplugging. They understand, and it gives me permission to unplug.

I inform my staff that I might not respond until the following day if they email me in the evening. I let them know I am always available via text messaging. I tell them that if it is urgent, they can call me. Explaining and modeling this system allowed my teachers to take time for themselves in the evening and not answer emails.

> *"Yesterday, I had staff coming up to me asking if I saw the email they sent Friday night or over the weekend. I have no problem telling them, 'Nope, I didn't check any emails this weekend.' Then I go into what I did with my family and friends. It's important to let them know to unplug for themselves as well."*
>
> Mr. Michael Earnshaw
> Elementary School Principal, Chicago, IL

The tickler file

I first heard of this system at a conference in 2007. The plan was created by extremely busy individuals who must attend to many tasks and meet deadlines. The presenter at the conference shared how he uses The Tickler File to help manage his daily routines. He uses 31 folders, each labeled to correspond to a day of the month. Here is how I use this system.

- I arrive at work and take out the file for that day.

- Inside, I have reminders of what I need to do that day. These tasks could include meetings, phone calls, or cards to write for staff birthdays.
- When I receive information about a future meeting, I place it in the appropriate folder. This system automatically organizes all pertinent information.

The system is simple yet powerful.

Seek out other methods that work for your colleagues

As you know, educators are often the best thieves. We beg, borrow, or steal anything and everything we can. Did you ever think that Teachers Pay Teachers, an online marketplace for original educational resources, would be mentioned in the same breath as a curriculum resource?

Mr. John Hinds encouraged me to read Dave Ellis's book *Falling Awake*. The book examines goal setting and living a whole life in a one-sentence summary. My biggest takeaway from the book is carrying index cards everywhere I go. The index cards allowed me to make notes on the observations, ideas, to-dos, or quotes I wanted to remember. If I noticed that a wall in a wing of campus needed to be cleaned or painted, I wrote that on an index card. When I returned to the office, I could give this index card to either the head custodian or the assistant principal in charge of facilities. It truly helped keep me organized and remember what needed to be done.

During my first few years, I carried a notebook with me. I have known administrators who use the note feature on their phones to record their to-do lists. I also took photos of tasks that needed to be done as I wandered my campus.

Former principal Shane Mckay leads a school of over 3,000 students and 300 staff members. He said, "I calendar everything and let my secretary manage my calendar." Mr. Mckay subscribes to The Breakthrough Coach's time management philosophy. The system maintains that with their method, you can reduce most administrators' workloads by 15-20 hours a week (YES, PER WEEK) and increase their classroom time by 500%. An average principal uses The Breakthrough Coaching model to spend 18 hours weekly in classrooms. Let me say that again: 18 hours a week are spent in classrooms. The key to this philosophy is utilizing the principal's secretary. The secretary controls the principal's calendar. Mr. Mckay also meets with his secretary first thing in the morning to discuss the day and weeks to come. If you are reading this and you are spinning or feeling overwhelmed, then your system isn't working, and you need to find a plan that works.

I have received advice from mentors throughout the years, which allowed me to develop my blueprint for time management. This plan allows me to manage my day.

I love to read about great coaches, and Nick Saban from the University of Alabama is an excellent study of leadership. In a day and age where college football is experiencing great parity, the Crimson Tide has been the class of college football for the last decade.

> *"I didn't invent any of this stuff. I learned it from somebody. So, I always look for the next guy I will learn from."*
>
> Nick Saban
University of Alabama

Don't let your pride get in the way of searching for systems to help you manage your day. If Nick Sabin is constantly working to ensure he is at the top of his game, it should be easy for us to do the same.

3. FIND JOY IN YOUR JOB

At one point, I was really struggling at work. I was negative and tired and everything was piling up on me. I will be the first to admit I needed to follow my blueprint for caring for myself.

Joaquin Hernandez, a principal in San Antonio, challenged me to get into classrooms and "find my joy." He reminded me that I needed to find what made me happy at work. That morning, I spent time in my special education classrooms. The students often bring joy to me.

If I continued to look for the negative aspects of the job, I would find them. The easiest way to find joy is by spending time with students during the day. If you consider why we became educators, it revolves around being with children. The further we move up the career ladder, the further and further away we get from working with children if we are not careful. We must purposefully plan to be around kids to avoid straying from them.

I bet every student and parent knew I was the principal on every campus I have led. Every student, parent, and teacher knew I cared about them because I intentionally spent quality time in the classroom and associated with students and teachers. At one point, I was giving a tour to prospective parents who were deciding on their child's school options. After the tour, the mom told me, "When I was in high school, I didn't even know what my principal looked like. I don't think I ever saw him." This was sad to hear.

When days are tough, I ensure I spend time in the cafeteria. I find a table of students to sit at and talk with. I ask for advice on my fantasy football team or what TV shows I should binge-watch. I never viewed cafeteria duty as just one more thing to do. Any opportunity to be around students is a privilege and should fill your bucket!

As a former coach, I enjoy seeing students excel in extracurricular activities. As a high school administrator, I sneak out and watch volleyball, basketball, or football practice during the day. Sometimes, as I watched, I would interact with the athletes or simply gather my thoughts and allow the students' efforts to put a smile on my face. I might even try to shoot a basket with the kids or hit a softball.

Frequently, administrators only get to deal with students in their office when they are in trouble. When I get bogged down with negativity, I call students to the office for positive visits. These can be students on an athletic team, who were in the school play, won an award at the science competition, or kids you just want to meet. Your school is filled with so many outstanding students that you can name dozens of students who fit this description off the top of your head. I know many schools that have successfully implemented the positive referral system.

During my second year as a middle school principal, I gave every student (almost 1,250 students) a handwritten birthday card on or as close to their birthday as I could. I would call them into the office and visit with them. This practice was highly time-consuming and one that I could only continue for a year, but it was rewarding and brought joy to my day.

I also found joy in sitting on benches during athletic events. It gave me a unique perspective on students and coaches, and it brought me joy.

Nothing brings more fun to the job than watching teachers in action. On tough days, watching an Algebra I teacher or a Chemistry teacher conduct an engaging lesson brings great joy to my day. I have also found that your irreplaceable teachers receive as much joy and pleasure from your visit as you do. Dr. Bobby Martinez finds joy in his job by strategically scheduling time to visit classrooms.

"At least two days per week (Tuesday and Thursday), I do my best to avoid placing things on my calendar. These days are designated to instruction and being in classrooms. I make it a point to be visible and encourage staff to invite me to any lessons they want me to participate in. There are also the days when I'll grab a novel our students are reading and head into an ELA classroom to sit and read."

Dr. Bobby Martinez
Assistant Superintendent of Secondary Education,
Alvin, TX

The job is challenging, and it has only gotten more so. I honestly don't see the pressures subsiding anytime soon. But one thing is in our control. I encourage you to schedule time in your day to find joy in your school.

What I would do differently if I started my principalship today

To use a runner's analogy, the principalship is a marathon. Yet, we try to run it at a sprinter's pace. This is illogical, and nobody can win with that approach to the long game. Dr. Alex Flores, Executive Director of Region 20 Educational Service Center, believes, "We are the victims of the bar we set." When we begin our job, we want to be everywhere. We want the dance team to know we are there for them as much as for the speech and debate team. What about the wrestling team or the student who invites you to his Eagle Scout ceremony?

If you are a high school administrator, out-of-city travel for teams and groups is monthly. If you are not careful, you spend the weekend supporting your school teams in various cities. Remember, all this time away comes at the expense of your family.

Frederick C. Buskey, an educational consultant, believes, "I can't do everything! Therefore, I have to choose what gets done. My choices reflect my values. It is brutal and liberating simultaneously, but it helps place purposeful work above urgent work."

Another thing is learning to take a C for a grade. There are many tasks where okay is good enough – just check the box and move on. Perfection is dangerous to emotional and physical health.

If I could start over again, I would…

1. Not arrive before 6:30 am each day.
2. Use more of my personal, vacation, and sick days throughout the year.
3. Attend games, activities & concerts but leave once they start.
4. Remove email from my phone permanently.
5. Make exercise part of my daily and weekly routine.
6. NEVER miss a family function. EVER!
7. Delegate more.
8. Say "No" more.
9. Take my advice more!
10. Realize the school won't crumble if I'm not there.

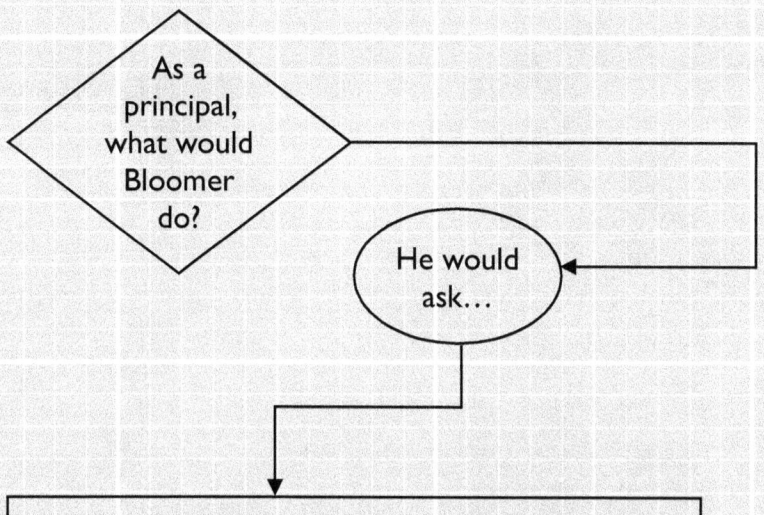

- What change can you make to your routine that would put your life and work balance into proper perspective?
- What is one example of the joy you found this week? How can you create more opportunities to find joy?

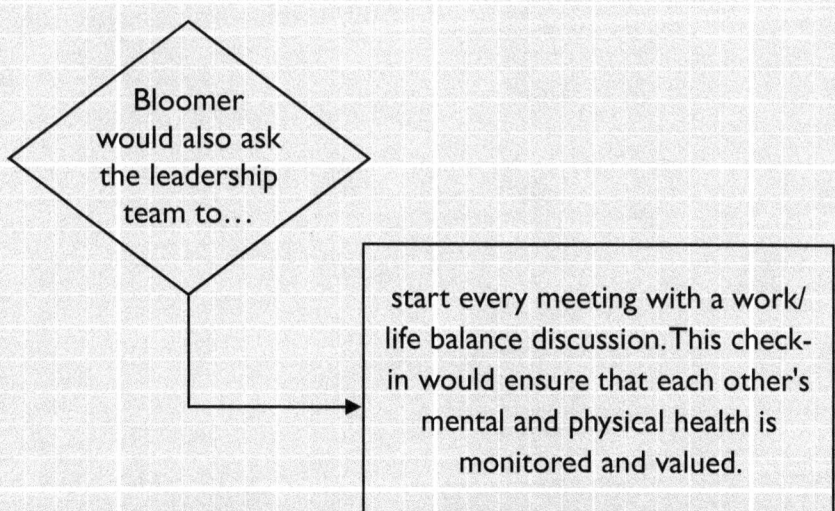

CHAPTER 7
Advice for Administrators
Don't Take My Advice
Take Theirs

"I would tell a brand new principal to actively manage the school's reputation. Making deposits into the 'reputation account' will allow for withdrawals later in a crisis, controversy, or turmoil. It may seem daunting to manage a reputation on top of everything else a new principal has on their plate, but it's much easier to do that than to repair a reputation when it's damaged. It can take years to rebuild 'reputation capital' once lost.

Here's the good news – people want to help with this. Every campus has a natural set of cheerleaders -- people who are enthusiastic about your school and willing to cheer about it. It may be a combination of staff and parents, but all are ready and willing to help. I think the RootEd representatives are an excellent example of that. A principal just needs to empower those cheerleaders within a set of expectations.

A business can achieve its objectives more easily if it has a good reputation among its stakeholders, especially key stakeholders such as its largest customers, opinion leaders in the business community, suppliers, and current and potential employees.

Don't you think that rings true for a principal, too? I've never been in your shoes, so I'm making some assumptions, but if your legacy families and most vocal PTA parents have your back, doesn't it help you fulfill your goals and objectives a bit easier?

My background is in public relations, so that's the lens through which I see the world. If you care for your people, they'll care for you."

Deb Caldwell
Director of Public Relations North East ISD
San Antonio, TX

"You have made me a better leader because of the administrator you are. You challenge me to better myself daily. You must have your staff buy into your philosophies and be willing to work diligently with a great leadership team that will spread your positive thoughts throughout the campus. With these people beside you, you can create an inviting workplace for the staff and students. Be ready to adjust to situations because they always arise. Last, have an open-door policy with your staff."

Rene Truan
Teacher/Coach San Antonio, TX

"It's okay to take time for yourself. As a mother who had two little ones under two years of age, recently built a new home, was in her doctoral program (finished in two years from the UT CSP), and was trying to run a high school, I think taking time for yourself as an individual and being revitalized is/was critical. Lean on your mentors and be transparent to do what is best.

Connecting with people during work and life is not easy, but it is well worth it. Show off what your staff and students do. Give people grace. Look for people's strengths and build from those. Visit and see other campuses and districts; visit with fellow principals in their schools. I visited Todd many moons ago, and it was so good for my soul, my campus, and the students/staff I have served. Focus on the good. Reach out; we're all in this together, and any position has a lot of negativity. Principalship can be all-consuming, so be true to yourself, make mistakes, apologize, and move forward. The best of your days are ahead, and the kids are worth it. Teachers are worth it. Get into the classrooms and be engaged in the actual work. It's a pleasure and joy; enjoy it, and keep your chin up. We're all rooting for you."

Dr. Lindsie Almquist
Wife, Mom, Executive Director
of School Leadership and Campus Support

"As a first-year principal, it is crucial to understand that the culture and climate of your school are foundational to its successes. Start by actively listening and engaging with all members of the school community - students, teachers, staff, and parents – to gain a comprehensive understanding of their experiences and expectations. Remember, a positive climate not only enhances academic outcomes but also promotes the well-being and growth of the entire school community."

Dominic Armano
Principal, Lincoln Avenue Elementary School,
Sayville Public Schools, Sayville, NY

"I've only been a teacher for four years, and I truly believe I have had the privilege to work for the best principal in Texas. I have been involved in sports since I was very young, so I have had the opportunity to grow under many leaders. Out of all my years of being an athlete, I have never had anyone like my past principal challenge and encourage me to grow in a way that is not only the best for me but, most importantly, the best for me to impact others. Seeing how much he cared for the staff and students brought about this growth in me. Having a principal who can run the school well and with authority is important, but I think having a principal who genuinely cares for the entire school is far more important. He had a passion for doing his job well and cared about the students and staff, which was evident in how visible he was on campus. He made it a priority to be seen around the school to build relationships with students and staff. He cared enough to look at the little details around the school. As John Wooden said, 'Little things make big things happen.' Once you start paying attention to the little things, big things happen around the school. Having a leader who is not afraid to do the *small* jobs or the jobs that technically don't have to be done by the leader and could be assigned to someone below him are the things that make a BIG difference. All these things created a ripple effect on our campus. When you see your principal cares, you care. When you see your principal picking up trash, you pick up trash because you care about your campus. When you see your principal go out of his way to speak to a student, you then go out of your way to speak to a student. I could keep giving you examples of what a great leader looks like because, as I said, I have had the opportunity to grow under a great leader, and not a day goes by that I don't try harder for my students.

So, what do I want from a principal? I want a principal who is passionate about their job, students, and staff more than anything. When you care and take the time to develop relationships with students and staff when discipline is necessary, the students realize that you care about them. When principals care deeply for their schools, they are respected and appreciated by the students and staff. High expectations for students and staff make everyone want to do their best. I promise you that if you work for someone on fire for their job, you will grow in ways you never thought possible. And isn't that what we need in this day and age of teaching? Someone who causes you to grow so you can encourage your students and impact them to grow and care for others."

Courtney Johnson
Coach, San Antonio, TX

"I have been a principal for ten years -- at different campuses in different districts. Circumstances, contexts, expectations, personalities, goals, systems, and dynamics can all make the principalship different. Still, some things about the principalship are true whether you've been in it for a week or a decade, regardless of the campus and district. It's both rewarding and heartbreaking; it highlights your inadequacies as much as it relies on your strengths and the seep-into-your-bones all-consuming. Constant contact with those currently fighting the good fight of the principalship is the only way to navigate the intricacies of this role: talking about it with your principal tribe, seeking out other principals around the world through social media and networking and, yes, reading about it, will help you reconcile those nagging fears, feel empowered to try those big ideas, and remind you that the fight is GOOD. And nobody better invigorates you to stay in it than the others in it, too."

Lindsay Harris
Georgetown ISD, TX

"In my experience as a student under five different principals, outreach to students is critical, especially at the middle and high school levels. A personable principal who seeks constant advice or counsel from individual students will always be able to feel how well the students are getting along. It is important to understand how involved some students are and how others wish to get more involved. Showing individualized support for clubs and organizations by approving and engaging in those activities goes a long way. Each time Mac Teach or PALS has a new event, Mr. Davidson and Mr. Schwartz harp on getting backing and support from the administration to participate. Safety and guidelines must be followed, especially by someone in such a high position. Still, the events that benefit the school community, feeder schools, and project partner organizations should always be considered.

Also, I've grown quite close to many teachers I respect greatly, and they seem to envision an ideal principal who empathetically understands the teacher's dedication to their students' success.

Colby Mask
Student, San Antonio, TX

While I never had the opportunity to serve as a principal, I learned something about leadership on a different level while serving at the district level. I think it would transfer to the principalship...

Get to know your campus. Know how the entire machine works. You don't have to have a deep level of understanding, but as the campus leader you should know the parts, components, and function of your entire campus. Know your counselors, and the value-add they bring to your students. Know the night custodial crew, and recognize their value. Which rooms are in the worst condition? Which rooms are farthest from the restrooms? The knowledge you have when you truly know your campus can come into play in many decisions that you make. This also can allow you to have empathy when listening to faculty/staff concerns.

Ben Peterson
Former Administrator/Central Office Leader
San Antonio, TX

What are some of the characteristics you feel a good principal has? A strong campus principal excels by casting a clear and inspiring vision that guides the entire school community toward shared goals. They are consistently visible, engaging with students, teachers, and parents alike, fostering a sense of unity and trust. Moreover, they recognize and appreciate the value of all stakeholders, ensuring that every voice is heard and respected, which cultivates an inclusive and supportive educational environment.

Advice to a 1st-year Principal: As a first-year administrator remember to ask questions, as you won't always have the answers. Admitting when you make a mistake and learning from it demonstrates your authenticity and fosters trust. Invest in all types of relationships, from cafeteria workers and janitors to teachers, parents, and secretaries, to build a supportive community. Use your calendar for everything and set alarms as reminders to stay organized. Most importantly, show yourself grace – it's a year of learning! Have a blast!!!

Lilly Caloway
Administrator Churchill High School

"When you were a teacher, students looked to you for guidance, for support. Now that you are principal, many look to you for guidance, support, and a safe place – students, teachers, staff, parents, and the community. You must remember it's not about perfection. This essential work requires tremendous grace and compassion and always doing what is best for kids. This is not an easy position. Not everyone will like you or some of the decisions you have to make. But at the end of the day or the end of your principal journey, I hope you will walk away with trust and respect. Trust and respect that you have offered to those around you and trust and respect that was offered to you."

Michelle Poteet
Parent

"Dear new principal: you are the leader of a great place – your school. Before school, walk the halls with your coffee, popping into classrooms to ask your teachers what they are teaching and wish them a great day. Be visible out in the halls during passing periods, talking to students. Hold teachers and students accountable for rules, procedures, and expectations that are important to you and the district. Be firm and forgiving. Listen to your teacher leaders and support them when they firmly believe in something. Be proud of the school you lead, and let it show through your visibility."

Maria Rodriguez
Teacher, San Antonio, TX

"My husband's job resulted in us moving quite a bit. This resulted in me teaching in three states, and I've had SEVEN principals over the past 14 years... so I've seen quite a range over time.

As a teacher, I want a principal who focuses on connecting with staff, parents, and students. This principal should be highly visible around the building, coming into classrooms, greeting the students at the door, sometimes doing cafeteria duty, and making meaningful connections with the school community. Significant work may occur in the office or behind closed doors, but a more favorable impression is made when you are seen frequently for informal interactions.

Compassion and confidentiality go hand in hand. I relate these two ideas to staff. The stressors and pressures accompanying classroom teaching can affect a teacher's health. We will all face challenging team situations, personal difficulties at home, or job frustrations during our career that we may choose to communicate to our principal. When the staff comes to you with these problems, you must focus your response on being compassionate. Nothing is worse than wanting to be heard only to have your concerns or situation downplayed or even one-upped. Even more critical is the need to keep information like this confidential. You may want to discuss the matter with others on your admin team, but sometimes, some information just doesn't need to be shared. Once this type of confidentiality is lost, it is hard to regain the trust of your staff."

Daliene Hendon
Teacher, San Antonio, TX

"Honestly, show them [teachers] that you are there for them to continue their education journey. Get out of your office, and see what is happening in your school." Corey Boe, @CorBoe5

"Create an atmosphere of excellence by leading with your arm around shoulders rather than your hand around necks, and use the EIEIO principle – Encourage, Inspire, Empower, Invest uplifting words, Overcome negatives with positives." Ron Lewis, @rhlewisbooks

"Being fake is detectable by your staff: fake smiles, fake concern, fake… doesn't build a great school climate, but tears it down. Admit failure and work on improving or correcting it." Bonnie T., @kd5lri

"Be genuine with your teachers! Let them see you take risks! Support them! Stand up for your beliefs! SHARE! Learn and grow together! Teachers will do their personal best when they know you are doing your personal best." Janet Gonzales, @chanagonzales

"Everyone on your team matters! The students, parents, support staff, maintenance staff, and teachers all want to know that you value them and they are important to you. What a blessing you are to touch the lives of so many around you." Amanda Cooper, @amandAVCooper

"Value the voices of both teachers and students. Ask teachers what they love about the school. Also, ask them if they could change something, what would it be, and why. And then really lean in and listen. Same with students." Tina McCorkle, @mccorkle_tina

"Visit classrooms regularly so you never forget how hard teachers work and how much they sacrifice for their students." Kelly Cross, @kcross34

"Give your teachers the benefit of the doubt. Assume their goal is excellence, and always support them on that journey." Danny Steele, @steelethoughts

FAREWELL →

Thank you very much for reading *The Blueprint*. This project has been like a family member. I have watched it grow, been frustrated, and loved it dearly. It is part of my family and always will be.

I would like to thank a few exceptional people who helped complete this project:

Ms. Linda Steitle is one of the best English teachers I have ever worked with and my main editor. Disclaimer – any errors discovered were my fault.

My friends, for wearing *The Blueprint* shirts and helping share my work

I hope that something from *The Blueprint* makes you a better administrator. I wish you the best and know you will be the difference maker that your community needs.

Thanks again,
Todd Bloomer

About the Author

Originally from New York, Todd Bloomer now calls San Antonio, Texas his home. During his 28 years of service to public education, Todd has held numerous roles, including teacher, coach, assistant principal, and middle school principal. For the past five and a half years, he has been the principal of a large public high school in San Antonio. Todd embodies the spirit of Teddy Roosevelt's famous "Man in the Arena" speech. The fact that Todd is still in the arena after leading schools before, during, and after the COVID-19 pandemic, gives his voice credibility. He still faces the daily challenges that all administrators have to address.

Todd and his wonderful wife, Sharon, live in the community he serves with all five of his children, all of whom have attended and graduated from the high school he leads. He takes great pride in shopping at the same grocery store as his students.

How To Book Bloomer

Todd Bloomer is a highly sought-after speaker, coach, and consultant. He can tailor his presentations, keynote addresses, and coaching sessions to meet your specific needs. To set up a time to discuss how he can help you develop a blueprint for a successful school year or for more information, use the info below to contact him:

> https://toddmbloomer.com
> X - @bloomer_sa
> Linkedin @toddbloomer

More Books From Road To Awesome

Taking the Leap: A Field Guide for Aspiring School Leaders by Robert F. Breyer

Transform: Techy Notes to Make Learning Sticky by Debbie Tannenbaum

Becoming Principal: A Leadership Journey & The Story of School Community by Dr. Jeff Prickett

Elevate Your Vibe: Action Planning with Purpose by Lisa Toebben

#OwnYourEpic: Leadership Lessons in Owning Your Voice and Your Story by Dr. Jay Dostal

The Design Thinking, Entrepreneurial, Visionary Planning Leader: A Practical guide for Thriving in Ambiguity by Dr. Michael Nagler

Becoming the Change: Five Essential Elements to Being Your Best Self by Dan Wolfe

inspired: moments that matter by Melissa Wright

Foundations of Instructional Coaching: Impact People, Improve Instruction, Increase Success by Ashley Hubner

Out of the Trenches: Stories of Resilient Educators
by Dana Goodier

Principled Leader
by Bobby Pollicino

Road to Awesome: The Journey of a Leader
by Darrin Peppard

When Calling Parents Isn't Your Calling: A teacher's guide to communicating with all parents
by Crystal Frommert

Struggle to Strength: Finding the Ingredients to Your Secret Sauce
by Kip Shubert

Guiding Transformational Change in Education
by Kristina V. Mattis

Be the Cause: An Educator's Guide to EFFECTive Instruction
by Josh Korb

https://roadtoawesome.net/books

KID'S BOOKS FROM ROAD TO AWESOME

Road to Awesome A Journey for Kids
by Jillian DuBois and Darrin M. Peppard

Emersyn Blake and the Spotted Salamander
by Kim Collazo

Theodore Edward Makes a New Friend
by Alyssa Schmidt

I'm Autistic and I'm Awesome
by Derek Danziger

Emersyn Blake and the Stalked Jellyfish
by Kim Collazo

Birdie & Mipps
by Barbara Gruener

www.ingramcontent.com/pod-product-compliance
Lightning Source LLC
Chambersburg PA
CBHW071943160426
43198CB00011B/1527